Aug 1977

To Karen & Joel

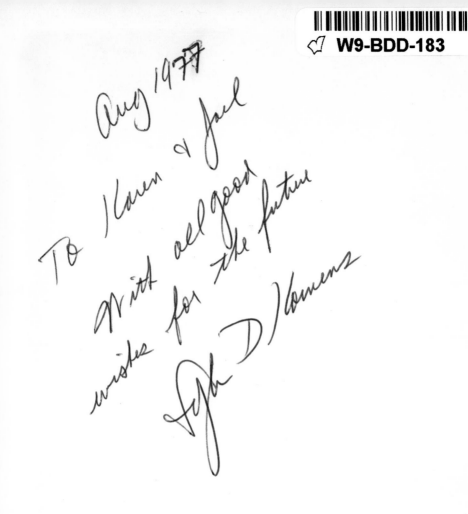

With all good wishes for the future

John D Kamens

THE BOOK OF PSALMS

ספר תהלים

The Book of Psalms

ספר תהלים

A New Translation
According to the Traditional
Hebrew Text

The Jewish Publication Society of America
Philadelphia

First edition, second impression 1975

ISBN 0–8276–0008–9
Library of Congress Catalog Card Number: 72–87909
Manufactured in the United States of America
Designed by Ismar David

PREFACE TO THE PSALMS TRANSLATION

In 1966 the Jewish Publication Society set up a committee of translators for the Ketubim, comprising professors Moshe Greenberg of the University of Pennsylvania (now of the Hebrew University), Jonas C. Greenfield of the University of California (now of the Hebrew University), and Nahum M. Sarna of Brandeis University, and associated with them rabbis Saul Leeman, Martin Rozenberg, and David Shapiro of the three sections of organized religious Jewish life in America. Dr. Chaim Potok, editor of the Society, served as secretary of the committee.

This English rendering of Psalms, the committee's first work, is a new version, not a revision of an earlier translation. It is based on the received (Masoretic) Hebrew text—its consonants, vowels, and syntactical divisions, although on occasion the traditional accentuation has been disregarded in favor of an alternative construction of a verse that appeared to yield a better sense. Such departures from the accentuation were made by many earlier Jewish commentators and translators.

The entire gamut of Psalms interpretation, from ancient to modern times, Jewish and non-Jewish, has been consulted. The results of modern study of the languages and cultures of the ancient Near East have been brought to bear on the biblical word wherever possible. In judging between alternatives, however, just as antiquity was not in itself a disqualification, so modernity was not in itself a recommendation. When the present translation diverges from recent renderings (as it frequently does), this is due as much to the committee's judgment that certain innovations, though interesting, are too speculative for adoption in the present state of knowledge, as to its commitment to the received Hebrew text (a commitment not made by most recent translations).

For many passages, our as yet imperfect understanding of the language of the Bible or what appears to be some disorder in the Hebrew text makes sure translation impossible. The committee's uncertainty is indicated in a marginal note, and alternative renderings have sometimes been offered where the Hebrew permits them. However, emendations of the text have not been proposed. Marginal annotations have been kept to a minimum since a companion volume of explanatory notes is in preparation.

The style of the translation is, on the whole, modern literary English. An effort has been made to retain the imagery of the Hebrew rather than to render it by English equivalents and approximations alien to the biblical world.

Consistency in rendering Hebrew terms was an aim but not an unqualified rule. Where its employment would have resulted in encumbered or awkward language it was abandoned. On the other hand, within a given psalm, key or thematic words and phrases were, as far as possible, rendered consistently. Repetition of key or thematic terms is an element of structure and composition in the psalms; its representation is one of the proper tasks of a translator. Terms having many values, such as *ḥesed* and *ṣedeq* (in the King James version, "mercy/lovingkindness" and "righteousness") posed a problem. In order to do justice to their wide range, a variety of renderings determined by the various contexts had to be employed. Here consistency was neither possible nor desirable.

The translators know that they have not conveyed the fullness of the Hebrew, with its ambiguities, its overtones, and the richness of meaning it carries from centuries of use. They do hope to have transmitted something of the directness, the simplicity, and the peculiarly Israelite expression of piety that are so essential to the sublimity of the Hebrew psalms.

ספר תהלים

THE BOOK OF PSALMS

BOOK ONE

1 Happy is the man who has not followed the counsel of the wicked,
or taken the path of sinners,
or joined the company of the insolent;
2 rather, his concern is the teaching of the LORD,
and he studies[a] that teaching day and night.
3 He is like a tree planted beside streams of water,
that yields its fruit in season,
whose foliage never fades,
and whatever [b-]it produces thrives.[-b]

4 Not so the wicked;
rather, they are like chaff that wind blows away.
5 Therefore the wicked will not survive judgment,
nor will sinners, in the assembly of the righteous.
6 For the LORD cherishes the way of the righteous,
but the way of the wicked is doomed.

[a] *Or "recites"*

[b-b] *Or "he does prospers"*

2 Why do nations assemble,
and peoples plot[a] vain things;
2 kings of the earth take their stand,
and regents intrigue together
against the LORD and against His anointed?
3 "Let us break the cords of their yoke,
shake off their ropes from us!"

4 He who is enthroned in heaven laughs;
the Lord mocks at them.
5 Then He speaks to them in anger,
terrifying them in His rage,
6 "But I have installed My king
on Zion, My holy mountain!"
7 Let me tell of the decree:
the LORD said to me,
[b-]"You are My son,
I have fathered you this day.[-b]
8 Ask it of Me,
and I will make the nations your domain;

[a] *Lit. "utter"*

[b-b] *Comp. II Sam. 7.14, and Ps. 89.27 f.*

your estate, the limits of the earth.
9 You can smash them with an iron mace,
shatter them like potter's ware."

10 So now, O kings, be prudent;
accept discipline, you rulers of the earth!
11 Serve the Lord in awe;
[c-]tremble with fright,[-c]
12 [d-]pay homage in good faith,[-d]
lest He be angered, and your way be doomed
in the mere flash of His anger.
Happy are all who take refuge in Him.

c-c Meaning of Heb uncertain; others "rejoice with trembling"
d-d Meaning of Heb uncertain

3

A psalm of David
when he fled from his son Absalom.

2 O LORD, my foes are so many!
Many are those who attack me;
3 many say of me,
"There is no deliverance for him from God." *Selah*
4 But You, O LORD, are a shield about me,
my glory, He who holds my head high.
5 I cry aloud to the LORD,
and He answers me from His holy mountain. *Selah*
6 I lie down and sleep and wake again,
for the Lord sustains me.
7 I have no fear of the myriad forces
arrayed against me on every side.

8 Rise, O LORD!
Deliver me, O my God!
For You slap all my enemies in the face;[a]
You break the teeth of the wicked.
9 Deliverance is the LORD's;
Your blessing be upon Your people! *Selah*

a Lit. "cheek"

4

[a-]For the leader; with instrumental music.[-a]
A psalm of David.

a-a Meaning of Heb uncertain

2 Answer me when I call,
O God, my vindicator!
You free me from distress;
have mercy on me and hear my prayer.

3 You men, how long will my glory be mocked,
will you love illusions,
have recourse to frauds? *Selah*
4 Know that the LORD singles out the faithful for Himself;
the LORD hears when I call to Him.
5 So tremble, and sin no more;
ponder it on your bed, and sigh.[b] *Selah*
6 Offer sacrifices in righteousness
and trust in the LORD.

[b] *Others "be still"*

7 Many say, "O for good days!"
[c-]Bestow Your favor on us,[-c] O LORD.
8 You put joy into my heart
when their grain and wine show increase.
9 Safe and sound, I lie down and sleep,
[d-]for You alone, O LORD, keep me secure.[-d]

[c-c] *Others "Lift up the light of Your countenance upon us"; cf. Num. 6.25 f.*

[d-d] *Or "for You, O LORD, keep me alone and secure"*

5

[a-]For the leader; on *nehiloth*.[-a]
A psalm of David.

[a-a] *Meaning of Heb uncertain*

2 Give ear to my speech, O LORD;
consider my utterance.
3 Heed the sound of my cry,
my king and God,
for I pray to You.
4 Hear my voice, O LORD, at daybreak;
at daybreak I plead before You, and wait.

5 For You are not a god who desires wickedness;
evil cannot abide with You;
6 wanton men cannot endure in Your sight.
You detest all evildoers;
7 You doom those who speak lies;
murderous, deceitful men the LORD abhors.

8 But I, through Your abundant love, enter Your house;
I bow down in awe at Your holy temple.
9 O LORD, [b-]lead me along Your righteous [path][-b]
because of my watchful foes;
make Your way straight before me.
10 For there is no sincerity on their lips;[c]
their heart is [filled with] malice;
their throat is an open grave;
their tongue slippery.

[b-b] *Or "as You are righteous, lead me"*

[c] *Lit. "mouth"*

11 Condemn them, O God;
let them fall by their own devices;
cast them out for their many crimes,
for they defy You.
12 But let all who take refuge in You rejoice,
ever jubilant as You shelter them;
and let those who love Your name exult in You.
13 For You surely bless the righteous, O LORD,
encompassing him with favor like a shield.

6

[a]-For the leader; with instrumental music on the *sheminith*.-[a]
A psalm of David.

[a-a] *Meaning of Heb uncertain*

2 O LORD, do not punish me in anger,
do not chastise me in fury.
3 Have mercy on me, O LORD, for I languish;
heal me, O LORD, for my bones shake with terror.
4 My whole being is stricken with terror,
while You, LORD—O, how long!
5 O LORD, return! rescue me!
Deliver me as befits Your faithfulness.
6 For there is no praise of You among the dead;
in Sheol, who can acclaim You?

7 I am weary with groaning;
every night I drench my bed,
I melt my couch in tears.
8 My eyes are wasted by vexation,
worn out because of all my foes.
9 Away from me, all you evildoers,
For the LORD heeds the sound of my weeping.
10 The LORD heeds my plea,
the LORD accepts my prayer.
11 All my enemies will be frustrated and stricken with terror;
they will turn back instantly, frustrated.

7

[a]-*Shiggaion* of David,-[a] which he sang to the LORD,
concerning Cush, a Benjaminite.

[a-a] *Meaning of Heb uncertain*

2 O LORD, my God, in You I seek refuge;
deliver me from all my pursuers and save me,
3 lest, like a lion they tear me apart,
rending in pieces, and no one save me.

4 O Lord, my God, if I have done such things,
if my hands bear the guilt of wrongdoing,
5 if I have dealt evil to my ally,
—[b]I who rescued my foe without reward[b]—
6 then let the enemy pursue and overtake me;
let him trample my life to the ground,
and lay my body in the dust. *Selah*

b-b Meaning of Heb uncertain; others "Or stripped my foe clean"

7 Rise, O Lord, in Your anger;
assert Yourself [c]against the fury of my foes;[c]
bestir Yourself on my behalf;
You have ordained judgment.
8 [a]Let the assembly of peoples gather about You,
with You enthroned above, on high.[a]
9 The Lord judges the peoples;
vindicate me, O Lord,
for the righteousness and blamelessness that are mine.
10 Let the evil of the wicked come to an end,
but establish the righteous;
he who probes the mind and conscience[d] is God the righteous.
11 [e]I look to God to shield me;[e]
the deliverer of the upright.
12 God vindicates the righteous;
God [f]pronounces doom[f] each day.
13 [g]If one does not turn back, but whets his sword,
bends his bow and aims it,
14 then against himself he readies deadly weapons,
and makes his arrows sharp.[g]
15 See, he hatches evil, conceives mischief,
and gives birth to fraud.
16 He has dug a pit and deepened it,
and will fall into the trap he made.
17 His mischief will recoil upon his own head;
his lawlessness will come down upon his skull.
18 I will praise the Lord for His righteousness,
and sing a hymn to the name of the Lord, most high.

c-c Or "in Your fury against my foes"

a-a Meaning of Heb uncertain

d Lit. "kidneys"

e-e Cf. Ibn Ezra and Kimhi; lit. "My shield is upon God"

f-f Others "has indignation"

g-g Meaning of vv. 13–14 uncertain; an alternate rendering, with God as the main subject, is:
13 If one does not turn back, He whets His sword,
bends His bow and aims it;
14 deadly weapons He prepares for him,
and makes His arrows sharp

8

[a]For the leader; on the *gittith.*[a]
A psalm of David.

2 O Lord, our Lord,
How majestic is Your name throughout the earth,
[b]You who have covered the heavens with Your splendor![b]
3 [a]From the mouths of infants and sucklings

a-a Meaning of Heb uncertain

b-b Meaning of Heb uncertain; or "You whose splendor is celebrated all over the heavens"

You have founded strength on account of Your foes,
to put an end to enemy and avenger.-[a] *[a-a] Meaning of Heb uncertain*
4 When I behold Your heavens, the work of Your fingers,
the moon and stars that You set in place:
5 what is man that You have been mindful of him,
mortal man that You have taken note of him,
6 that You have made him little less than divine,[c] *[c] Or "the angels"*
and adorned him with glory and majesty;
7 You have made him master over Your handiwork,
laying the world at his feet,
8 sheep and oxen, all of them,
and wild beasts, too,
9 the birds of the heavens, the fish of the sea,
whatever travels the paths of the seas.
10 O LORD, our Lord, how majestic is Your name throughout the earth!

9

[a]-For the leader; *'almuth labben.*-[a]
A psalm of David.

[a-a] Meaning of Heb uncertain; some mss. and ancient versions, "'al muth"

2 I will praise You, LORD, with all my heart;
I will tell all Your wonders.
3 I will rejoice and exult in You,
singing a hymn to Your name, O Most High.

4 When my enemies retreat,
they stumble to their doom at Your presence.
5 For You uphold my right and claim,
enthroned as righteous judge.
6 You blast the nations;
You destroy the wicked;
You blot out their name forever.
7 [b]-The enemy is no more—
ruins everlasting;
You have torn down their cities;
their very names are lost.-[b] *[b-b] Meaning of Heb uncertain*
8 But the LORD abides forever;
He has set up His throne for judgment;
9 it is He who will judge the world with righteousness,
rule the peoples with equity.
10 The LORD is a haven for the oppressed,
a haven in times of trouble.
11 Those who know Your name trust You,
for You do not abandon those who turn to You, O LORD.

12 Sing a hymn to the LORD, [c-]who reigns in Zion;[-c]
declare His deeds among the peoples.
13 [d-]For He does not ignore the cry of the afflicted;
He who requites bloodshed is mindful of them.[-d]
14 Have mercy on me, O LORD;
see my affliction at the hands of my foes,
You who lift me from the gates of death,
15 so that in the gates of [e-]Fair Zion[-e]
I might tell all Your praise,
I might exult in Your deliverance.
16 The nations sink in the pit they have made;
their own foot is caught in the net they have hidden.
17 The LORD has made Himself known:
He works judgment;
the wicked man is snared by his own devices. *Higgaion. Selah*
18 Let the wicked be[f] in Sheol,
all the nations who ignore God!
19 Not always shall the needy be ignored,
nor the hope of the afflicted forever lost.
20 Rise, O LORD!
Let not men have power;
let the nations be judged in Your presence.
21 [b-]Strike fear into them,[-b] O LORD;
let the nations know they are only men. *Selah*

c-c Or "O You who dwell in Zion"

d-d Order of Hebrew clauses inverted for clarity

e-e Lit. "the Daughter of Zion"

f Others "return to"

b-b Meaning of Heb uncertain

10

Why, O LORD, do You stand aloof,
heedless in times of trouble?
2 The wicked in his arrogance hounds the lowly—
[a-]may they be caught in the schemes they devise![-a]
3 [b-]The wicked crows about his unbridled lusts;
the grasping man reviles and scorns the LORD.
4 The wicked, arrogant as he is,
in all his scheming [thinks],
"He does not call to account;
God does not care."[-b]
5 His ways prosper at all times;
Your judgments are far beyond him;
he snorts at all his foes.
6 He thinks, "I shall not be shaken,
through all time never be in trouble."
7 His mouth is full of oaths, deceit and fraud;
mischief and evil are under his tongue.
8 He lurks in outlying places;
from a covert he slays the innocent;

a-a Or "they (i.e. the lowly) are caught by the schemes they devised"

b-b Meaning of Heb uncertain

his eyes spy out the hapless.
9 He waits in a covert like a lion in his lair;
waits to seize the lowly;
he seizes the lowly as he pulls his net shut;
10 he stoops, he crouches,
[b]-and the hapless fall prey to his might.-[b]
11 He thinks, "God is not mindful,
He hides His face, He never looks."
12 Rise, O LORD!
[c]-Strike at him,-[c] O God!
Do not forget the lowly.
13 Why should the wicked man scorn God,
thinking You do not call to account?
14 You do look!
You take note of mischief and vexation!
[b]-To requite is in Your power.-[b]
To You the hapless can entrust himself;
You have ever been the orphan's help.
15 O break the power of the wicked and evil man,
so that when You [d]-look for-[d] his wickedness
You will find it no more.

b-b Meaning of Heb uncertain

c-c Lit. "Lift Your hand"

d-d A play on darash, *which in vv. 4, 13 means "to call to account"*

16 The LORD is king forever and ever;
the nations will perish from His land.
17 You will listen to the entreaty of the lowly, O LORD,
You will make their hearts firm;
You will incline Your ear
18 to champion the orphan and the downtrodden,
[b]-that men who are of the earth tyrannize no more.-[b]

11 For the leader.
[A psalm] of David.

In the LORD I take refuge;
how can you say to me,
"Take to [a]-the hills like a bird!-[a]
2 For see, the wicked bend the bow,
they set their arrow on the string
to shoot from the shadows at the upright.
3 [b]-When the foundations are destroyed,
what can the righteous do?"-[b]

4 The LORD is in His holy palace;
the LORD—His throne is in heaven;

a-a Meaning of Heb uncertain; lit. "your hill, bird!"

b-b Or "For the foundations are destroyed; what has the Righteous One done?" Or "If the foundations are destroyed, what has the righteous accomplished?"

His eyes behold, His gaze searches mankind.
5 The LORD seeks out the righteous,
but loathes the wicked who loves injustice.
6 He will rain down upon the wicked blazing coals and sulphur;
a scorching wind shall be [c]-their lot.-[c]
7 For the LORD is righteous;
He loves righteous deeds;
the upright shall behold His face.

[c-c] *Lit. "the portion of their cup"*

12 For the leader; [a]-on the *sheminith*.-[a]
A psalm of David.

[a-a] *Meaning of Heb uncertain*

2 Help, O LORD!
For the faithful are no more;
the loyal have vanished from among men.
3 Men speak lies to one another;
their speech is smooth;
they talk with duplicity.
4 May the LORD cut off all flattering lips,
every tongue that speaks arrogance.
5 They say, "By our tongues we shall prevail;
with lips such as ours, who can be our master!"

6 "Because of the groans of the plundered poor and needy,
I will now act," says the LORD.
[a]-"I will give help," He affirms to him.-[a]
7 The words of the LORD are pure words,
silver purged in an earthen crucible,
refined sevenfold.
8 You, O LORD, will keep them,
guarding each [a]-from this age-[a] evermore.
9 On every side the wicked roam
[a]-when baseness is exalted among men.-[a]

13 For the leader.
A psalm of David.

2 How long, O LORD, will You forever ignore me?
How long will You hide Your face from me?
3 How long will I have cares on my mind,
grief in my heart all day?
How long will my enemy have the upper hand?
4 Look at me, answer me, O LORD, my God!

[a-]Restore my strength,[-a]
lest I sleep the sleep of death;
5 lest my enemy say, "I have overcome him,"
my foes exult when I totter.
6 But I trust in Your faithfulness,
my heart will exult in Your deliverance.
I will sing to the LORD,
for He has been good to me.

a-a Lit. "Give light to my eyes"; cf. I Sam. 14.27–30; Ps. 38.11; Ezra 9.8

14[a]

For the leader.
[A psalm] of David.

a Cf. Psalm 53

The benighted man thinks,
[b-]"God does not care."[-b]
Man's deeds are corrupt and loathsome;
no one does good.
2 The LORD looks down from heaven on mankind
to find a man of understanding,
a man mindful of God.
3 All have turned bad,
altogether foul;
there is none who does good,
not even one.
4 Are they so witless, all those evildoers,
who devour my people as they devour food,
and do not invoke the LORD?
5 There they will be seized with fright,
for God is present in the circle of the righteous.
6 You may set at nought the counsel of the lowly,
but the LORD is his refuge.

b-b Lit. "There is no God"

7 O that the deliverance of Israel might come from Zion!
When the LORD restores the fortunes of His people,
Jacob will exult, Israel will rejoice.

15

A psalm of David.

LORD, who may stay in Your tent,
who may reside on Your holy mountain?
2 He who lives without blame,
who does what is right,
and in his heart acknowledges the truth;
3 [a-]whose tongue is not given to evil;[-a]

a-a Meaning of Heb uncertain; or "Who has no slander upon his tongue"

who has never done harm to his fellow,
or borne reproach for [his acts toward] his neighbor;
4 for whom a contemptible man is abhorrent,
but who honors those who fear the LORD;
who stands by his oath even to his hurt;
5 who has never lent money at interest,
or accepted a bribe against the innocent;
the man who acts thus shall never be shaken.

16 A *miktam*[a] of David.

Protect me, O God, for I seek refuge in You.
2 I say to the LORD,
"You are my Lord, [b-]my benefactor;
there is none above You."[-b]
3 [c-]As to the holy and mighty ones that are in the land,
my sole concern about them is that
4 those who espouse another [god]
may have many sorrows![-c]
I will have no part of their bloody libations;
their names will not pass my lips.
5 The LORD is my alloted share and portion;[d]
You control my fate.
6 My lot has fallen in delightful country,
lovely indeed is my estate.
7 I bless the LORD who has guided me;
my conscience[e] admonishes me at night.
8 I am ever aware of the LORD's presence;
He is at my right hand; I shall never be shaken.
9 So my heart rejoices,
my whole being exults,
and my body rests secure.
10 For You will not abandon me to Sheol,
or let Your faithful one see the Pit.
11 You will teach me the path of life.
In Your presence is perfect joy;
delights are ever in Your right hand.

[a] *Meaning of Heb uncertain*

[b-b] *Others "I have no good but in You"*

[c-c] *Meaning of Heb uncertain; "holy and mighty ones" taken as divine beings; cf.* qedoshim *in Ps. 89.6, 8, and* adirim *in I Sam. 4.8*

[d] *Lit. "cup"*

[e] *Lit. "kidneys"*

17 A prayer of David.

Hear, O LORD, what is just;
heed my cry, give ear to my prayer,
uttered without guile.

2 My vindication will come from You;
Your eyes will behold what is right.
3 You have visited me at night, probed my mind,
You have tested me and found nothing amiss;
[a-]I determined that my mouth should not transgress.
4 As for man's dealings,
in accord with the command of Your lips,[-a]
I have kept in view the fate[b] of the lawless.
5 My feet have held to Your paths;
my legs have not given way.

[a-a] *Meaning of Heb uncertain*

[b] *Cf. Prov. 1.19; lit. "paths"*

6 I call on You;
You will answer me, God;
turn Your ear to me,
hear what I say.
7 Display Your faithfulness in wondrous deeds,
You who deliver with Your right hand
those who seek refuge from assailants.
8 Guard me like the apple of Your eye;
hide me in the shadow of Your wings
9 from the wicked who despoil me,
[c-]my mortal enemies who[-c] encircle me.
10 [a-]Their hearts are closed to pity;[-a]
they mouth arrogance;
11 now they hem our feet on every side;
they set their eyes roaming over the land.
12 He is like a lion eager for prey,
a king of beasts lying in wait.

[c-c] *Or "from my enemies who avidly"*

13 Rise, O LORD! Go forth to meet him.
Bring him down;
rescue me from the wicked with Your sword,
14 [a-]from men, O LORD, by Your hand,
from men whose share in life is fleeting.
But as to Your treasured ones,
fill their bellies.[-a]
Their sons too shall be satisfied,
and have something to leave over for their young.
15 Then I, justified, will behold Your face;
awake, I am filled with the vision of You.

18[a]

For the leader.
[A psalm] of David, the servant of the LORD, who
addressed the words of this song to the LORD
after the LORD had saved him from the hands
of all his enemies and from the clutches of Saul.
2 He said:
[b-]I adore you, O LORD, my strength,[-b]
3 O LORD, my rock, my fortress, my rescuer,
my God, my shelter in whom I seek refuge,
my shield, [c-]my mighty champion,[-c] my haven.
4 [d-]All praise! I called on the LORD[-d]
and was delivered from my enemies.
5 Bonds[e] of Death encompassed me;
torrents of Belial terrified me;
6 bonds of Sheol encircled me;
snares of Death confronted me.
7 In my distress I called on the LORD,
cried out to my God;
in His temple He heard my voice;
my cry to Him reached His ears.
8 Then the earth rocked and quaked;
the foundations of the mountains shook,
rocked by His indignation;
9 smoke went up from His nostrils,
from His mouth came devouring fire;
live coals blazed forth from Him.
10 He bent the sky and came down,
thick cloud beneath His feet.
11 Mounted on a cherub, He flew,
gliding on the wings of the wind.
12 He made darkness His screen;
dark thunderheads, dense clouds of the sky,
were His pavilion round about Him.
13 Out of the brilliance before Him,
hail and fiery coals [f-]pierced His clouds.[-f]
14 Then the LORD thundered from heaven,
the Most High gave forth His voice—
[g-]hail and fiery coals.[-g]
15 He let fly His shafts and scattered them;
He discharged lightning and routed them.
16 The ocean bed was exposed;
the foundations of the world were laid bare
by Your mighty roaring, O LORD,
at the blast of the breath of Your nostrils.

[a] *This poem occurs again as II Sam. 22, with a number of variations, some of which are cited in the following notes*

[b-b] *Not in II Sam. 22.2*

[c-c] *Lit. "the horn of my help"*

[d-d] *Construction of Heb uncertain*

[e] *II Sam. 22.5, "Breakers"*

[f-f] *II Sam. 22.13, "did blaze"*

[g-g] *Not in II Sam. 22.14*

17 He reached down from on high, He took me;
He drew me out of the mighty waters;
18 He saved me from my fierce enemy,
from foes too strong for me.
19 They confronted me on the day of my calamity,
but the LORD was my support.
20 He brought me out to freedom;
He rescued me because He was pleased with me.

21 The LORD rewarded me according to my merit;
He requited the cleanness of my hands;
22 for I have kept to the ways of the LORD,
and have not been guilty before my God;
23 for I am mindful of all His rules;
I have not disregarded His laws.
24 I have been blameless toward Him,
and have guarded myself against sinning;
25 and the LORD has requited me according to my merit,
the cleanness of my hands in His sight.

26 With the loyal, You deal loyally;
with the blameless man, blamelessly.
27 With the pure, You act purely,
and with the perverse, You are wily.
28 It is You who deliver lowly folk,
but haughty eyes You humble.
29 It is You who light my lamp;
the LORD, my God, lights up my darkness.
30 With You, I can rush a barrier;[h]
with my God I can scale a wall;
31 the way of God is perfect;
the word of the LORD is pure;
He is a shield to all who seek refuge in Him.
32 Truly, who is a god except the LORD,
who is a rock but our God?—
33 the God who girded me with might,
who made my way perfect;
34 who made my legs like a deer's,
and let me stand firm on the[i] heights;
35 who trained my hands for battle;
my arms can bend a bow of bronze.
36 You have given me the shield of Your protection;
Your right hand has sustained me,
Your care[j] has made me great.
37 You have let me stride on freely;

[h] *Or "troop"*

[i] *Taking* bamothai *as a poetic form of* bamoth; *cf. Hab. 3.19; others "my"*

[j] *Meaning of Heb uncertain; others "condescension"*

my feet have not slipped.
38 I pursued my enemies and overtook them;
I did not turn back till I destroyed them.
39 I struck them down,
and they could rise no more;
they lay fallen at my feet.
40 You have girded me with strength for battle,
brought my adversaries low before me,
41 made my enemies turn tail before me;
I wiped out my foes.
42 They cried out, but there was none to deliver;
[cried] to the LORD, but He answered them not.
43 I ground them fine as windswept dust;
I trod them flat as the dirt of the streets.
44 You have rescued me from the strife of people;
You have set me at the head of nations;
peoples I knew not must serve me.
45 At the mere report of me they are submissive;
foreign peoples cower before me;
46 foreign peoples lose courage,
[k-]and come trembling out of their strongholds.[-k]

[k-k] *Meaning of Heb uncertain*

47 The LORD lives! Blessed is my rock!
Exalted be God, my deliverer,
48 the God who has vindicated me
and made peoples subject to me,
49 who rescued me from my enemies,
who raised me clear of my adversaries,
saved me from lawless men.
50 For this I sing Your praise among the nations, LORD,
and hymn Your name.
51 [l-]He accords great victories[-l] to His king,
keeps faith with His anointed,
with David and his offspring forever.

[l-l] *II Sam. 22.51, "Tower of Victory"*

19

For the leader.
A psalm of David.

2 The heavens declare the glory of God,
the sky proclaims His handiwork;
3 Day to day makes utterance,
night to night speaks out.
4 There is no utterance,
there are no words,

[a-]whose sound goes unheard.[-a]
5 Their voice[b] carries throughout the earth,
their words to the end of the world.
He placed in them[c] a tent for the sun,
6 who is like a groom coming forth from the chamber,
like a hero, eager to run his course.
7 His rising-place is at one end of heaven,
and his circuit reaches the other;
nothing escapes his heat.

8 The teaching of the LORD is perfect,
renewing life;
the decrees of the LORD are enduring,
making the simple wise;
9 The precepts of the LORD are just,
rejoicing the heart;
the instruction of the LORD is lucid,
[d-]restoring strength.[-d]
10 The fear of the LORD is pure,
abiding forever;
the judgments of the LORD are true,
righteous altogether,
11 more desirable than gold,
than much fine gold;
sweeter than honey,
than [e-]drippings of the comb.[-e]
12 Your servant pays them heed;
in obeying them there is much reward.
13 Who can be aware of errors?
Clear me of unperceived guilt,
14 and from [f-]willful sins[-f] keep Your servant;
let them not dominate me;
then shall I be blameless
and clear of grave offense.
15 May the words of my mouth
and the prayer of my heart
be acceptable to You,
O LORD, my rock and my redeemer.

[a-a] With Septuagint, Symmachus, and Vulgate; or "Their sound is not heard"

[b] Cf. Septuagint, Symmachus, and Vulgate; Arabic qawwa, *"to shout"*

[c] Viz. the heavens

[d-d] Cf. 13.4, note a-a

[e] Meaning of Heb uncertain

[f-f] Or "arrogant men"

20

For the leader.
A psalm of David.

2 The LORD answer you in time of trouble,
the name of Jacob's God keep you safe.

3 May He send you help from the sanctuary,
and sustain you from Zion.
4 May He receive the tokens[a] of all your meal offerings,
and approve[b] your burnt offerings. *Selah*
5 May He grant you your desire,
and fulfill your every plan.
6 May we shout for joy in your victory,
arrayed by standards in the name of our God.
May the LORD fulfill your every wish.

[a] *Reference to* azkara, *"token portion," of meal offering; Lev. 2.2, 9, 16, etc.*
[b] *Meaning of Heb uncertain*

7 Now I know that the LORD will give victory to His anointed,
will answer him from His heavenly sanctuary
with the mighty victories of His right arm.
8 They [call] on chariots, they [call] on horses,
but we call on the name of the LORD our God.
9 They collapse and lie fallen,
but we rally and gather strength.
10 [c]O LORD, grant victory!
May the King answer us when we call.[c]

[c-c] *Or, in the light of v. 7, "O LORD, grant victory to the king, may He answer us when we call"*

21

For the leader.
A psalm of David.

2 O LORD, the king rejoices in Your strength;
how greatly he exults in Your victory!
3 You have granted him the desire of his heart,
have not denied the request of his lips. *Selah*
4 You have proffered him blessings of good things,
have set upon his head a crown of fine gold.
5 He asked You for life; You granted it;
a long life, everlasting.
6 Great is his glory through Your victory;
You have endowed him with splendor and majesty.
7 You have made him blessed forever,
gladdened him with the joy of Your presence.
8 For the king trusts in the LORD;
Through the faithfulness of the Most High
he will not be shaken.
9 Your hand is equal to all Your enemies;
Your right hand overpowers Your foes.
10 You set them ablaze like a furnace
[a]when You show Your presence.[a]
The LORD in anger destroys them;
fire consumes them.

[a-a] *Or, "at the time of Your anger"*

11 You wipe their offspring from the earth,
their issue from among men.
12 For they schemed against You;
they laid plans,
but could not succeed.
13 [b]For You make them turn back[b]
by Your bows aimed at their face.
14 Be exalted, O LORD, through Your strength;
we will sing and chant the praises of Your mighty deeds.

[b-b] *Heb uncertain*

22 For the leader; on [a]*ayyeleth ha-shahar.*[a] A psalm of David.

[a-a] *Meaning of Heb uncertain*

2 My God, my God,
why have You abandoned me;
why so far from delivering me
and from my anguished roaring?
3 My God,
I cry by day—You answer not,
by night, and have no respite.

4 [b]But You are the Holy One,
enthroned,
the Praise of Israel.[b]
5 In You our fathers trusted,
they trusted, and You rescued them.
6 To You they cried out,
and they escaped;
in You they trusted,
and were not disappointed.

[b-b] *Or "But You are holy, enthroned upon the praises of Israel"*

7 But I am a worm, less than human;
scorned by men, despised by people.
8 All who see me mock me;
[c]they curl their lips,[c]
they shake their heads:
9 "Let him commit himself to the LORD;
let Him rescue him,
let Him save him,
for He is pleased with him."
10 You [a]drew me[a] from the womb,
made me secure at my mother's breast.
11 I became Your charge at birth;
from my mother's womb You have been my God.

[c-c] *Lit. "they open wide with a lip"*

12 Do not be far from me,
for trouble is near,
and there is none to help.
13 Many bulls surround me,
mighty bulls of Bashan encircle me.
14 They open their mouths at me
like tearing, roaring lions.
15 [d-]My life ebbs away:[-d]
All my bones are disjointed;
my heart is like wax,
melting within me;
16 my vigor dries up like a shard;
my tongue cleaves to my palate;
You commit me to the dust of death.
17 Dogs surround me;
a pack of evil ones closes in on me,
[e-]like lions [they maul] my hands and feet.[-e]
18 I take the count of all my bones
while they look on and gloat.
19 They divide my clothes among themselves,
casting lots for my garments.

20 But You, O LORD, be not far off;
my strength, hasten to my aid.
21 Save my life from the sword,
my precious life[f] from the clutches of a dog.
22 Deliver me from a lion's mouth;
from the horns of wild oxen rescue[g] me.
23 Then will I proclaim Your fame to my brethren,
praise You in the congregation.

24 You who fear the LORD, praise Him!
All you offspring of Jacob, glorify Him!
Be in dread of Him, all you offspring of Israel!
25 For He did not scorn, He did not spurn
the plea[h] of the lowly;
he did not hide His face from him;
when he cried out to Him, He listened.
26 [i-]Because of You I offer praise[-i] in the great congregation;
I pay my vows in the presence of His worshipers.
27 Let the lowly eat and be satisfied;
let all who seek the LORD praise Him.
Always be of good cheer!
28 Let all the ends of the earth pay heed and turn to the LORD,
and the peoples of all nations prostrate themselves before You;

[d-d] Lit. "I am poured out like water"

[e-e] With Rashi; cf. Isa. 38.13

[f] Lit. "only one"

[g] Lit. "answer"

[h] Or "plight"

[i-i] Lit. "From You is my praise"

29 for kingship is the LORD's
and He rules the nations.
30 [j]All those in full vigor shall eat and prostrate themselves;
all those at death's door, whose spirits flag,
shall bend the knee before Him.[j]
31 Offspring shall serve Him;
the LORD's fame shall be proclaimed to the generation
32 to come;
they shall tell of His beneficence
to people yet to be born,
for He has acted.

j-j Meaning of Heb uncertain; others "All the fat ones of the earth shall eat and worship; All they that go down to the dust shall kneel before Him, Even he that cannot keep his soul alive"

23 A psalm of David.

The LORD is my shepherd;
I lack nothing.
2 He makes me lie down in green pastures;
He leads me to [a]water in places of repose;[a]
3 He renews my life;
He guides me in right paths
as befits His name.
4 Though I walk through [b]a valley of deepest darkness,[b]
I fear no harm, for You are with me;
Your rod and Your staff—they comfort me.

5 You spread a table for me in full view of my enemies;
You anoint my head with oil;
my drink is abundant.
6 Only goodness and steadfast love shall pursue me
all the days of my life,
and I shall dwell in the house of the LORD
for many long years.

a-a Others "still waters"

b-b Others "the valley of the shadow of death"

24 A psalm of David.

The earth is the LORD's and all that it holds,
the world and its inhabitants.
2 For He founded it upon the ocean,
set it on the nether-streams.
3 Who may ascend the mountain of the LORD?
Who may stand in His holy place?—
4 He who has clean hands and a pure heart,
who has not taken a false oath by My[a] life

a Ancient versions and some mss. read "His"

or sworn deceitfully.
5 He shall carry away a blessing from the LORD,
a just reward from God, his deliverer.
6 Such are the people[b] who turn to Him,
Jacob, who seek Your presence. *Selah*

[b] *Lit. "generation"*

7 O gates, lift up your heads!
Up high, you everlasting doors,
so the King of Glory may come in!
8 Who is the King of Glory?—
the LORD, mighty and valiant,
the LORD, valiant in battle.
9 O gates, lift up your heads!
Lift them up, you everlasting doors,
so the King of Glory may come in!
10 Who is the King of Glory?—
the LORD of hosts,
He is the King of Glory! *Selah*

25 [A psalm] of David.

א O LORD, I set my hope on You;
ב 2 my God, in You I trust;
may I not be disappointed,
may my enemies not exult over me.
ג 3 O let none who look to You be disappointed;
let the faithless be disappointed, empty-handed.
ד 4 Let me know Your paths, O LORD;
teach me Your ways;
הו 5 guide me in Your true way and teach me,
for You are God, my deliverer;
it is You I look to at all times.
ז 6 O LORD, be mindful of Your compassion,
and Your faithfulness;
they are old as time.
ח 7 Be not mindful of my youthful sins and transgressions;
in keeping with Your faithfulness consider what is in my favor,
as befits Your goodness, O LORD.
ט 8 Good and upright is the LORD;
therefore He shows sinners the way.
י 9 He guides the lowly in the right path,
and teaches the lowly His way.
כ 10 All the LORD's paths are steadfast love
for those who keep the decrees of His covenant.

ל 11 As befits Your name, O LORD,
pardon my iniquity though it be great.
מ 12 Whoever fears the LORD,
he shall be shown what path to choose.
נ 13 He shall live a happy life,
and his children shall inherit the land.
ס 14 The counsel[a] of the LORD is for those who revere Him;
to them he makes known His covenant.
ע 15 My eyes are ever toward the LORD,
for He will loose my feet from the net.
פ 16 Turn to me, have mercy on me,
for I am alone and afflicted.
צ 17 [b-]My deep distress[-b] increases;
deliver me from my straits.
ר 18 Look at my affliction and suffering,
and forgive all my sins.
19 See how numerous my enemies are,
and how unjustly they hate me!
ש 20 Protect me and save me;
let me not be disappointed,
for I have sought refuge in You.
ת 21 May integrity and uprightness watch over me,
for I look to You.
22 O God, redeem Israel
from all its distress.

[a] Or "secret"

[b-b] Lit. "The distress of my heart"

26 [A psalm] of David.

Vindicate me, O LORD,
for I have walked without blame;
I have trusted in the LORD;
I have not faltered.
2 Probe me, O LORD, and try me,
test my [a-]heart and mind;[-a]
3 [b-]for my eyes are on Your steadfast love;
I have set my course by it.[-b]
4 I do not consort with scoundrels,
or mix with hypocrites;
5 I detest the company of evil men,
and do not consort with the wicked;
6 I wash my hands in innocence,
and walk around Your altar,
7 raising my voice in thanksgiving,
and telling all Your wonders.

[a-a] Lit. "kidneys and heart"

[b-b] Or "I am aware of Your faithfulness, and always walk in Your true [path]"

8 O LORD, I love Your temple abode,
the dwelling-place of Your presence.
9 Do not sweep me away with sinners,
or [snuff out] my life with murderers,
10 who have schemes at their fingertips,
and hands full of bribes.
11 But I walk without blame;
redeem me, have mercy on me!
12 My feet are on level ground.
In assemblies I will bless the LORD.

27 [A psalm] of David.

The LORD is my light and my help;
whom should I fear?
The LORD is the stronghold of my life,
whom should I dread?
2 When evil men assail me
[a]to devour my flesh[a]—
it is they, my foes and my enemies,
who stumble and fall.
3 Should an army besiege me,
my heart would have no fear;
should war beset me,
still would I be confident.

4 One thing I ask of the LORD,
only that do I seek:
to live in the house of the LORD
all the days of my life,
to gaze upon the beauty of the LORD,
[b]to frequent[b] His temple.
5 He will shelter me in His pavilion
on an evil day,
grant me the protection of His tent,
raise me high upon a rock.
6 Now is my head high
over my enemies roundabout;
I sacrifice in His tent with shouts of joy,
singing and chanting a hymn to the LORD.

7 Hear, O LORD, when I cry aloud;
have mercy on me, answer me.
8 [b]In Your behalf[b] my heart says:

[a-a] *Or "to slander me"; cf. Daniel 3.8; 6.25*

[b-b] *Meaning of Heb uncertain*

"Seek My face!"
O LORD, I seek Your face.
9 Do not hide Your face from me;
do not thrust aside Your servant in anger;
you have ever been my help.
Do not forsake me, do not abandon me,
O God, my deliverer.
10 Though my father and mother abandon me,
the LORD will take me in.
11 Show me Your way, O LORD,
and lead me on a level path
because of my watchful foes.
12 Do not subject me to the will of my foes,
for false witnesses and unjust accusers
have appeared against me.
13 Had I not the assurance
that I would enjoy the goodness of the LORD
in the land of the living. . . .

14 Look to the LORD;
be strong and of good courage;
O look to the LORD!

28 [A psalm] of David.

O LORD, I call to You;
my rock, do not disregard me,
for if You hold aloof from me,
I shall be like those gone down into the Pit.
2 Listen to my plea for mercy
when I cry out to You,
when I lift my hands
toward Your inner sanctuary.
3 Do not [a]count me[a] with the wicked and evildoers
who profess goodwill toward their fellows
while malice is in their heart.
4 Pay them according to their deeds,
their malicious acts;
according to their handiwork pay them,
give them their deserts.
5 For they do not consider the LORD's deeds,
the work of His hands.
May He tear them down,
never to rebuild them!

[a-a] *Or "drag me off"; meaning of Heb uncertain*

6 Blessed is the LORD,
for He listens to my plea for mercy.
7 The LORD is my strength and my shield;
my heart trusts in Him.
I was helped,[b] and my heart exulted,
so I will glorify Him with my song.
8 The LORD is [c]their strength;[c]
He is a stronghold for the deliverance of His anointed.
9 Deliver and bless Your very own people;
tend them and sustain them forever.

[b] Or "strengthened"
[c-c] Greek, Saadia and others render, and some mss. read, oz le'ammo, *"the strength of His people"*

29 A psalm of David.

Ascribe to the LORD, O divine beings,
ascribe to the LORD glory and strength.
2 Ascribe to the LORD the glory of His name;
bow down to the LORD, majestic in holiness.
3 The voice of the LORD is over the waters;
the God of glory thunders,
the LORD, over the mighty waters.
4 The voice of the LORD is power;
the voice of the LORD is majesty;
5 the voice of the LORD breaks cedars;
the LORD shatters the cedars of Lebanon.
6 [a]He makes Lebanon skip like a calf,[a]
Sirion, like a young wild ox.
7 The voice of the LORD kindles flames of fire;
8 the voice of the LORD convulses the wilderness;
the LORD convulses the wilderness of Kadesh;
9 the voice of the LORD causes hinds to calve,
[b]and strips forests bare;[b]
while in His temple all say "Glory!"
10 The LORD sat enthroned at the Flood;
the LORD sits enthroned, king forever.

11 May the LORD grant strength to His people;
may the LORD bestow on His people well-being.

[a-a] Lit. "He makes them skip like a calf, Lebanon and Sirion, etc."
[b-b] Or "brings ewes to early birth"

30 A psalm of David.
A song for the dedication of the temple.[a]

2 I extol You, O LORD,
for You have lifted me up,

[a] So traditionally taken; lit. "house"

and not let my enemies rejoice over me.
3 O LORD, my God,
I cried out to You,
and You healed me.
4 O LORD, You brought me up from Sheol,
preserved me from going down into the Pit.

5 O you faithful of the LORD, sing to Him,
and praise His holy name.
6 For He is angry but a moment,
and when He is pleased there is life.
[b-]One may lie down weeping at nightfall;[-b]
but at dawn there are shouts of joy.

[b-b] Or "Weeping may linger for the night"

7 When I was untroubled,
I thought, "I shall never be shaken,"
8 for You, O LORD, when You were pleased,
made [me][c] firm as a mighty mountain.
When You hid Your face,
I was terrified.
9 I called to You, O LORD;
to my Lord I made appeal.
10 "What is to be gained from my death,[d]
from my descent into the Pit?
Can dust praise You?
Can it declare Your faithfulness?
11 Hear, O LORD, and have mercy on me;
O LORD, be my help!"

[c] Following Saadia, R. Isaiah of Trani; cf. Ibn Ezra

[d] Lit. "blood"

12 You turned my lament into dancing,
you undid my sackcloth and girded me with joy,
13 that [my] whole being might sing hymns to You endlessly;
O LORD my God, I will praise You forever.

31

For the leader.
A psalm of David.

2 I seek refuge in You, O LORD;
may I never be disappointed;
as You are righteous, rescue me.
3 Incline Your ear to me;
be quick to save me;
be a rock, a stronghold for me,
a citadel, for my deliverance.

4 For You are my rock and my fortress;
You lead me and guide me as befits Your name.
5 You free me from the net laid for me,
for You are my stronghold.
6 Into Your hand I entrust my spirit;
You redeem me, O LORD, faithful God.
7 I detest those who rely on empty folly,
but I trust in the LORD.
8 Let me exult and rejoice in Your faithfulness
in that You notice my affliction,
are mindful of my deep distress,
9 and do not hand me over to my enemy,
but [a-]grant me relief.[-a]

[a-a] *Lit. "make my feet stand in a broad place"*

10 Have mercy on me, O LORD,
for I am in distress;
my eyes are wasted by vexation,
[b-]my substance and body too.[-b]

[b-b] *Meaning of Heb uncertain*

11 My life is spent in sorrow,
my years in groaning;
my strength fails because of my iniquity,
my limbs waste away.
12 Because of all my foes,
I have become the butt of my neighbors,
a horror to my friends;
those who see me on the street avoid me.
13 I am put out of mind like the dead;
I am like an object given up for lost.
14 I hear the whisperings of many,
a terror on every side,
as they intrigue together against me,
plotting to take my life.

15 But I trust in You, O LORD;
I say, "You are my God!"
16 My fate is in Your hand;
save me from the hand of my enemies and pursuers.
17 Show favor to Your servant;
as You are faithful, deliver me.
18 O LORD, let me not be disappointed when I call You;
let the wicked be disappointed;
let them be silenced in Sheol;
19 let lying lips be stilled
that speak haughtily against the righteous
with arrogance and contempt.

20 How abundant is the good
that You have in store for those who fear You,
that You do in the full view of men,
for those who take refuge in You.
21 You grant them the protection of Your presence
[b]-against scheming men;-[b]
You shelter them in Your pavilion
from contentious tongues.
22 Blessed is the LORD,
for He was wondrously faithful to me,
a veritable bastion.
23 Alarmed, I had thought,
"I am thrust out of Your sight";
yet You listened to my plea for mercy
when I cried out to You.
24 So love the LORD, all you faithful;
the LORD guards the loyal,
and more than requites
him who acts arrogantly.
25 Be strong and of good courage,
all you who wait for the LORD.

b-b Meaning of Heb uncertain

32 [A psalm] of David.
[a]-A *maskil*.-[a]

a-a Meaning of Heb uncertain

Happy is he whose transgression is forgiven,
whose sin is covered over.
2 Happy the man whom the LORD does not hold guilty,
and in whose spirit there is no deceit.

3 As long as I said nothing,
my limbs wasted away
from my anguished roaring all day long.
4 For night and day
Your hand lay heavy on me;
my vigor waned
as in the summer drought. *Selah*
5 Then I acknowledged my sin to You;
I did not cover up my guilt;
I resolved, "I will confess my transgressions to the LORD,"
and You forgave the guilt of my sin. *Selah*
6 Therefore let every faithful man pray to You
[b]-upon discovering [his sin],-[b]
that the rushing mighty waters

b-b Meaning of Heb uncertain; others "In a time when You may be found"

not overtake him.
7 You are my shelter;
You preserve me from distress;
You surround me with the joyous shouts of deliverance. *Selah*

8 Let me enlighten you
and show you which way to go;
let me offer counsel; my eye is on you.
9 Be not like a brainless horse or mule
[a-]whose movement must be curbed by bit and bridle;[-a]
[c-]far be it from you![-c]
10 Many are the torments of the wicked,
but he who trusts in the LORD
shall be surrounded with favor.
11 Rejoice in the LORD and exult, O you righteous;
shout for joy, all upright men!

a-a Meaning of Heb uncertain

c-c Meaning of Heb uncertain; for this rendering cf. Ibn Ezra

33

Sing forth, O righteous, to the LORD;
it is fit that the upright acclaim Him.
2 Praise the LORD with the lyre;
with the ten-stringed harp sing to Him;
3 sing Him a new song;
play sweetly with shouts of joy.
4 For the word of the LORD is right
His every deed is faithful.
5 He loves what is right and just;
the earth is full of the LORD's faithful care.
6 By the word of the LORD the heavens were made,
by the breath of His mouth all their host.
7 He heaps up the ocean waters like a mound,
stores the deep in vaults.

8 Let all the earth fear the LORD;
let all the inhabitants of the world dread Him.
9 For He spoke, and it was;
He commanded, and it endured.
10 The LORD frustrates the plans of nations,
brings to nought the designs of peoples.
11 What the LORD plans endures forever,
what He designs, for ages on end.

12 Happy the nation whose God is the LORD,
the people He has chosen to be His own.
13 The LORD looks down from heaven;

He sees all mankind.
14 From His dwelling-place He gazes
on all the inhabitants of the earth—
15 He who fashions the hearts of them all,
who discerns all their doings.

16 A king is not delivered by a large force;
a warrior is not saved by great strength;
17 a horse is a false hope for deliverance;
for all its great power it provides no escape.
18 Truly the eye of the LORD is on those who fear Him,
who wait for His faithful care,
19 to save them from death,
to sustain them in famine.
20 We set our hope on the LORD,
He is our help and shield;
21 in Him our hearts rejoice,
for in His holy name we trust.
22 May we enjoy, O LORD, Your faithful care,
as we have put our hope in You.

34

[A psalm] of David,
[a-]when he feigned madness in the presence of Abimelech,
who turned him out, and he left.[-a]

[a-a] *Cf. I Sam. 21. 14*

א 2 I bless the LORD at all times;
praise of Him is ever in my mouth.
ב 3 I glory in the LORD;
let the lowly hear it and rejoice.
ג 4 Exalt the LORD with me;
let us extol His name together.
ד 5 I turned to the LORD, and He answered me;
He saved me from all my terrors.
ה 6 Men look to Him and are radiant;
ו let their faces not be downcast.
ז 7 Here was a lowly man who called,
and the LORD listened,
and delivered him from all his troubles.
ח 8 The angel of the LORD camps around those who fear Him
and rescues them.
ט 9 Taste and see how good the LORD is;
happy the man who takes refuge in Him!
י 10 Fear the LORD, you His consecrated ones,
for those who fear Him lack nothing.

כ 11 Lions have been reduced to starvation,
but those who turn to the LORD shall not lack any good.
ל 12 Come, my sons, listen to me;
I will teach you what it is to fear the LORD.
מ 13 Who is the man who is eager for life,
who desires years of good fortune?
נ 14 Guard your tongue from evil,
your lips from deceitful speech.
ס 15 Shun evil and do good,
seek amity and pursue it.
ע 16 The eyes of the LORD are on the righteous,
His ears attentive to their cry.
פ 17 The face of the LORD is against evildoers,
to erase their names from the earth.
צ 18 They[b] cry out, and the LORD hears,
and saves them from all their troubles.
ק 19 The LORD is close to the brokenhearted;
those crushed in spirit He delivers.
ר 20 Though the misfortunes of the righteous be many,
the LORD will save him from them all,
ש 21 Keeping all his bones intact,
not one of them being broken.
ת 22 One misfortune is the deathblow of the wicked;
the foes of the righteous shall be ruined.
23 The LORD redeems the life of His servants;
all who take refuge in Him shall not be ruined.

[b] *Viz. the righteous of v. 16*

35 [A psalm] of David.

O LORD, strive with my adversaries,
give battle to my foes,
2 take the shield and buckler,
and come to my defense;
3 ready the spear and javelin
against my pursuers;
tell me, "I am your deliverance."
4 Let those who seek my life
be frustrated and put to shame;
let those who plan to harm me
fall back in disgrace.
5 Let them be as chaff in the wind,
the LORD's angel driving them on.
6 Let their path be dark and slippery,
with the LORD's angel in pursuit.

7 For without cause they hid a net to trap me;
without cause they dug a pit[a] for me.
8 Let disaster overtake them unawares;
let the net they hid catch them;
let them fall into it when disaster [strikes].
9 Then shall I exult in the LORD,
rejoice in His deliverance.
10 All my bones shall say,
"LORD, who is like You,
who saves the poor from one stronger than he,
the poor and needy from his despoiler."

[a] Transferred from first clause for clarity

11 Malicious witnesses appear
who question me about things I do not know.
12 They repay me evil for good,
[seeking] my bereavement.
13 Yet, when they were ill,
my dress was sackcloth,
I kept a fast—
[b-]may what I prayed for happen to me![-b]
14 I walked about as though it were my bosom friend, my brother;
I was bowed with gloom, like one mourning for his mother.
15 But when I am stricken, they gleefully gather;
wretches gather against me,
I know not why;
[c-]they tear at me without end;
16 with impious, mocking grimace[-c]
they gnash their teeth at me.

[b-b] Meaning of Heb uncertain; lit. "my prayer returns upon my bosom"

[c-c] Meaning of Heb uncertain

17 O Lord, how long will You look on?
Rescue me [c-]from their attacks,[-c]
my precious life, from the lions,
18 that I may praise You in a great congregation,
acclaim You in a mighty throng.
19 Let not my enemies without cause rejoice over me,
or those who hate me without reason wink their eyes.
20 For they do not offer amity,
but devise treacherous schemes against harmless folk.
21 They open wide their mouths at me,
saying, "Aha, aha, we have seen it!"

22 You have seen it, O LORD;
do not hold aloof!
O Lord, be not far from me!
23 Wake, rouse Yourself for my cause,

for my claim, O my God and my Lord!
24 Take up my cause, O LORD my God, as You are beneficent,
and let them not rejoice over me.
25 Let them not think,
"Aha, just what we wished!"
Let them not say,
"We have destroyed him!"
26 May those who rejoice at my misfortune
be frustrated and utterly disgraced;
may those who vaunt themselves over me
be clad in frustration and shame.
27 May those who desire my vindication
sing forth joyously;
may they always say,
"Extolled be the LORD
who desires the well-being of His servant,"
28 while my tongue shall recite Your beneficent acts,
Your praises all day long.

36

For the leader.
For the servant of the LORD.
[A psalm] of David.

2 [a]I know[a] what Transgression says to the wicked;
he has no sense of the dread of God,
3 [b]because its speech is seductive to him
till his iniquity be found out and he be hated.[b]
4 His words are evil and deceitful;
he will not consider doing good.
5 In bed he plots mischief;
he is set on a path of no good,
he does not reject evil.

6 O LORD, Your faithfulness reaches to heaven;
Your steadfastness to the sky;
7 Your beneficence is like the high mountains;
Your justice like the great deep;
man and beast You deliver, O LORD.
8 How precious is Your faithful care, O God!
Mankind shelters in the shadow of Your wings.
9 They feast on the rich fare of Your house;
you let them drink at Your stream of delights.
10 With You is the fountain of life;
by Your light do we see light.

a-a *Lit. "In my heart is"*

b-b *Meaning of Heb uncertain*

11 Bestow Your faithful care on those devoted to You,
and Your beneficence on upright men.
12 Let not the foot of the arrogant tread on me,
or the hand of the wicked drive me away.
13 There will evildoers fall;
they will be thrust down, never to rise.

37 [A psalm] of David.

א Do not be vexed by evil men;
do not be incensed by wrongdoers;
2 for they soon wither like grass,
like verdure fade away.
ב 3 Trust in the LORD and do good,
abide in the land and remain loyal.
4 Urge your plea on the LORD,
and He will grant you the desires of your heart.
ג 5 Leave all[a] to the LORD;
trust in Him; He will do it.
6 He will cause your vindication to shine forth like the light,
the justice of your case, like the noonday sun.
ד 7 Be patient and wait for the LORD,
do not be vexed by the prospering man
who carries out his schemes.

ה 8 Give up anger, abandon fury,
do not be vexed;
it can only do harm.
9 For evil men will be cut off,
but those who look to the LORD—
they shall inherit the land.
ו 10 A little longer and there will be no wicked;
you will look at where he was—
he will be gone.
11 But the lowly shall inherit the land,
and delight in abundant well-being.
ז 12 The wicked man schemes against the righteous,
and gnashes his teeth at him.
13 The Lord laughs at him,
for He knows that his day will come.
ח 14 The wicked draw their swords, bend their bows,
to bring down the lowly and needy,
to slaughter [b-]upright men.[-b]

[a] *Lit. "your way"*

[b-b] *Lit. "those whose way is upright"*

ט 15 Their swords shall pierce their own hearts,
and their bows be broken.

16 Better the little that the righteous man has
than the great abundance of the wicked.

17 For the arms of the wicked shall be broken,
but the LORD is the support of the righteous.

י 18 The LORD is concerned for the needs[c] of the blameless;
their portion lasts forever;

19 they shall not come to grief in bad times;
in famine, they shall eat their fill.

[c] Lit. "days"

כ 20 But the wicked shall perish,
and the enemies of the LORD shall be consumed,
like meadow-grass[d] consumed in smoke.

[d] Meaning of Heb uncertain

ל 21 The wicked man borrows and does not repay;
the righteous is generous and keeps giving.

22 Those blessed by Him shall inherit the land,
but those cursed by Him shall be cut off.

מ 23 The steps of a man are made firm by the LORD,
when He delights in his way.

24 Should he stumble, he does not fall down,
for the LORD gives him support.

נ 25 I have been young and am now old,
but have yet to see a righteous man abandoned,
or his children seeking bread.

26 He is always generous, and lends,
and his children are held blessed.

ס 27 Shun evil and do good,
and you shall abide forever.

28 For the LORD loves what is right,
He does not abandon His faithful ones.
They are preserved forever,
while the children of the wicked will be cut off.

29 The righteous shall inherit the land,
and abide forever in it.

פ 30 The mouth of the righteous utters wisdom,
and his tongue speaks what is right.

31 The teaching of his God is in his heart;
his feet do not slip.

צ 32 The wicked watches for the righteous,
seeking to put him to death;

33 the LORD will not abandon him to his power;
He will not let him be condemned in judgment.

ק 34 Look to the LORD and keep to His way,
and He will raise you high that you may inherit the land;
when the wicked are cut off, you shall see it.

ר 35 I saw a wicked man in great power,
well-rooted like a robust native tree.
36 Suddenly he vanished and was gone;
I sought him, but he was not to be found.
ש 37 Mark the blameless, note the upright,
for there is a future for the man of integrity.
38 But transgressors shall be utterly destroyed,
the future of the wicked shall be cut off.
ת 39 But the deliverance of the righteous is from the LORD,
their stronghold in time of trouble.
40 The LORD helps them and rescues them,
rescues them from the wicked and delivers them,
for they seek refuge in Him.

38

A psalm of David.
Lehazkir.[a]

[a] *Meaning of Heb uncertain*

2 O LORD, do not punish me in wrath;
do not chastise me in fury.
3 For Your arrows have struck me;
Your blows have fallen upon me.
4 There is no soundness in my flesh because of Your rage,
no wholeness in my bones because of my sin.
5 For my iniquities have [b-]overwhelmed me;[-b]
they are like a heavy burden, more than I can bear.
6 My wounds stink and fester
because of my folly.
7 I am all bent and bowed;
I walk about in gloom all day long.
8 For my sinews are full of fever;
there is not a sound spot in my body.
9 I am all benumbed and crushed;
I roar because of the turmoil in my mind.

10 O Lord, You are aware of all my entreaties;
my groaning is not hidden from You.
11 My mind reels;
my strength fails me;
my eyes too have lost their luster.
12 My friends and companions stand back from my affliction;
my kinsmen stand far off.
13 Those who seek my life lay traps;
those who wish me harm speak malice;
they utter deceits all the time.

[b-b] *Lit. "passed over my head"*

14 But I am like a deaf man, unhearing,
like a dumb man who cannot speak up;
15 I am like one who does not hear,
who has no retort on his lips.
16 But I wait for You, O LORD;
You will answer, O Lord, my God.
17 For I fear they will rejoice over me;
when my foot gives way they will vaunt themselves against me.
18 For I am on the verge of collapse;
my pain is always with me;
19 I acknowledge my iniquity;
I am fearful over my sin;
20 for my mortal enemies are numerous;
those who hate me without cause are many.
21 Those who repay evil for good
harass me for pursuing good.

22 Do not abandon me, O LORD;
my God, be not far from me;
23 hasten to my aid,
O Lord, my deliverance.

39

For the leader; for Jeduthun.
A psalm of David.

2 I resolved I would watch my step
lest I offend by my speech;
I would keep my mouth muzzled,
while the wicked was in my presence.
3 I was dumb, silent;
I was very[a] still
while my pain was intense.
4 My mind was in a rage,
my thoughts were all aflame;
I spoke out:
5 Tell me, O LORD, what my term is,
what is the measure of my days;
I would know how fleeting my life is.
6 You have made my life just handbreaths long;
its span is as nothing in Your sight;
[b-]no man endures any longer than a breath.[-b] *Selah*
7 Man walks about as a mere shadow;
mere futility is his hustle and bustle,
amassing and not knowing who will gather in.

[a] *Cf. use of* ṭwb *in Micah 1.12; Jer. 15.11; Hos. 10.1; Jonah 4.4*

[b-b] *Meaning of Heb uncertain*

8 What, then, can I count on, O Lord?
In You my hope lies.
9 Deliver me from all my transgressions;
make me not the butt of the benighted.
10 I am dumb, I do not speak up,
for it is Your doing.
11 Take away Your plague from me;
I perish from Your blows.
12 You chastise a man in punishment for his sin,
consuming like a moth what he treasures.
No man is more than a breath. *Selah*

13 Hear my prayer, O LORD;
give ear to my cry;
do not disregard my tears;
for like all my forebears
I am an alien, resident with You.
14 Look away from me, that I may recover,
before I pass away and am gone.

40

For the leader.
A psalm of David.

2 I put my hope in the Lord;
He inclined toward me,
and heeded my cry.
3 He lifted me out of the miry pit,
the slimy clay,
and set my feet on a rock,
steadied my legs.
4 He put a new song into my mouth,
a hymn to our God.
May many see it and stand in awe,
and trust in the LORD.
5 Happy is the man who makes the LORD his trust,
who turns not to the arrogant or to followers of falsehood.
6 [a-]You, O LORD, my God have done many things;
the wonders You have devised for us
cannot be set out before You;[-a]
I would rehearse the tale of them,
but they are more than can be told.
7 [b-]You gave me to understand that[-b]
You do not desire sacrifice and meal offering;
You do not ask for burnt offering and sin offering.

[a-a] Or "You, O LORD, my God have done many things—the wonders You have devised for us; none can equal You!"

[b-b] Meaning of Heb uncertain

8 Then I said,
[b]"See, I will bring a scroll recounting what befell me."[b]
9 To do what pleases You, my God, is my desire;
Your teaching is in my inmost parts.
10 I proclaimed [Your] righteousness in a great congregation;
see, I did not withhold my words;
O LORD, You must know it.
11 I did not keep Your beneficence to myself;
I declared Your faithful deliverance;
I did not fail to speak of Your steadfast love in a great congregation.
12 O LORD, You will not withhold from me Your compassion;
Your steadfast love will protect me always.

b-b Meaning of Heb uncertain

13 For misfortunes without number envelope me;
my iniquities have caught up with me;
I cannot see;
they are more than the hairs of my head;
[c]I am at my wits' end.[c]
14[d] O favor me, LORD, and save me;
O LORD, hasten to my aid.
15 Let those who seek to destroy my life
be frustrated and disgraced;
let those who wish me harm
fall back in shame.
16 Let those who say "Aha! Aha!" over me
be desolate because of their frustration.
17 But let all who seek You be glad and rejoice in You;
let those who are eager for Your deliverance always say,
"Extolled be the LORD!"
18 But I am poor and needy;
may the Lord devise [deliverance] for me.
You are my help and my rescuer;
my God, do not delay.

c-c Or "my courage fails me"

d With vv. 14–18, cf. Ps. 70

41

For the leader.
A psalm of David.

2 Happy is he who is thoughtful of the wretched;
in bad times may the LORD keep him from harm.
3 May the LORD guard him and preserve him;
and may he be thought happy in the land.
Do not subject him to the will of his enemies.
4 The LORD will sustain him on his sickbed;
[a]You shall wholly transform his bed of suffering.[a]

a-a Meaning of Heb uncertain

5 I said, "O LORD, have mercy on me,
heal me, for I have sinned against You."
6 My enemies speak evilly of me,
"When will he die and his name perish?"
7 If one comes to visit, he speaks falsely;
his mind stores up evil thoughts;
once outside, he speaks them.
8 All my enemies whisper together against me,
imagining the worst for me.
9 "Something baneful has settled in him;
he'll not rise from his bed again."
10 My ally in whom I trusted,
even he who shares my bread,
[a]has been utterly false to me.[a]
11 But You, O LORD, have mercy on me;
let me rise again and repay them.
12 Then shall I know that You are pleased with me:
when my enemy cannot shout in triumph over me.
13 You will support me because of my integrity,
and let me abide in Your presence forever.

14 Blessed is the LORD, God of Israel,
from eternity to eternity.
Amen and Amen.

a-a Meaning of Heb uncertain

BOOK TWO

42

For the leader.
A *maskil* of the Korahites.

2 Like a hind crying for water,[a]
my soul cries for You, O God;
3 my soul thirsts for God, the living God;
O when will I come to appear before God!
4 My tears have been my food day and night;
I am ever taunted with "Where is your God?"
5 When I think of this, I pour out my soul:
how I [b]walked with the crowd, moved with them,[b]
the festive throng, to the house of God
with joyous shouts of praise.
6 Why so downcast, my soul,
why disquieted within me?

a Lit. "watercourses"

b-b Meaning of Heb uncertain

Have hope in God;
I will yet praise Him
[c]for His saving presence.[c]

[c-c] Several ancient versions and Heb. mss. connect the first word in v. 7 with the end of 6, reading yeshu'ot panai we'Elohai; *"my ever-present help, my God," as in vv. 12 and 43.5*

7 O my God, my soul is downcast;
therefore I think of You
in this land of Jordan and Hermon,
in Mount Mizar
8 where deep calls to deep
in the roar of [b]Your cataracts;[b]
all Your breakers and billows have swept over me.

[b-b] Meaning of Heb uncertain

9 By day may the LORD vouchsafe His faithful care,
that at night a song to Him may be with me,
a prayer to the God of my life.
10 I say to God, my rock,
"Why have You forgotten me,
why must I walk in gloom,
oppressed by my enemy?"
11 [b]Crushing my bones,[b]
my foes revile me,
taunting me always with "Where is your God?"
12 Why so downcast, my soul,
why disquieted within me?
Have hope in God;
I will yet praise Him,
my ever-present help, my God.

43 [a]

[a] A continuation of Ps. 42

Vindicate me, O God,
champion my cause
against faithless people;
rescue me from the treacherous, dishonest man.
2 For You are my God, my stronghold;
why have You rejected me?
Why must I walk in gloom,
oppressed by the enemy?
3 Send forth Your light and Your truth;
they will lead me;
they will bring me to Your holy mountain,
to Your dwelling-place,
4 that I may come to the altar of God,
God, my delight, my joy,
that I may praise You with the lyre,
O God, my God.
5 Why so downcast, my soul,

why disquieted within me?
Have hope in God;
I will yet praise Him,
my ever-present help, my God.

44

For the leader.
[A psalm] of the Korahites.
A *maskil.*

2 We have heard, O God,
our fathers have told us
the deeds You performed in their time,
in days of old.
3 With Your hand You planted them,
displacing nations;
You brought misfortune on peoples,
and drove them out.
4 It was not by their sword that they took the land,
their arm did not give them victory,
but Your right hand, Your arm, and Your goodwill,
for You favored them.
5 You are my king, O God;
decree victories for Jacob!
6 Through You we gore our foes;
by Your name we trample our adversaries;
7 I do not trust in my bow;
it is not my sword that gives me victory;
8 You give us victory over our foes;
You thwart those who hate us.
9 In God we glory at all times,
and praise Your name unceasingly. *Selah*

10 Yet You have rejected and disgraced us;
You do not go with our armies.
11 You make us retreat before our foe;
our enemies plunder us at will.
12 You let them devour us like sheep;
You disperse us among the nations.
13 You sell Your people for no fortune,
You set no high price on them.
14 You make us the butt of our neighbors,
the scorn and derision of those around us.
15 You make us a byword among the nations,
a laughingstock[a] among the peoples.

[a] *Lit. "a wagging of the head"*

16 I am always aware of my disgrace,
I am wholly covered with shame,
17 at the sound of taunting revilers,
in the presence of the vengeful foe.

18 All this has come upon us,
yet we have not forgotten You,
or been false to Your covenant.
19 Our hearts have not gone astray,
nor have our feet swerved from Your path,
20 though You cast us, crushed, to where the seamonster[b] is,
and covered us over with deepest darkness.
21 If we forgot the name of our God
and spread forth our hands to a foreign god,
22 God would surely search it out,
for He knows the secrets of the heart.
23 It is for Your sake that we are slain all day long,
that we are thought of as sheep to be slaughtered.

[b] *Heb.* tannim = tannin, *as in Ezek. 29.3 and 32.2*

24 Rouse Yourself, why do You sleep, O my Lord?
Awaken, do not reject us forever!
25 Why do You hide Your face,
ignoring our affliction and distress?
26 We lie prostrate in the dust;
our body clings to the ground.
27 Arise and help us,
redeem us, as befits Your faithfulness.

45

For the leader; [a]on *shoshannim.*[a]
A *maskil* of the Korahites.
A love song.

[a-a] *Meaning of Heb uncertain*

2 My heart is astir with gracious words;
I speak my poem to a king;
my tongue is the pen of an expert scribe.

3 You are fairer than all men;
your speech is endowed with grace;
rightly has God given you an eternal blessing.
4 Gird your sword upon your thigh, O hero,
in your splendor and glory;
5 [a]in your glory, win success;
ride on in the cause of truth and meekness and right;
and let your right hand lead you to awesome deeds.[a]

6 Your arrows, sharpened,
[b-][pierce] the breast of the king's enemies;
peoples fall at your feet.[-b]
7 Your [c-]divine throne[-c] is everlasting;
your royal scepter is a scepter of equity.
8 You love righteousness and hate wickedness;
rightly has God, your God, chosen to anoint you
with oil of gladness, over all your peers.
9 All your robes [are fragrant] with
myrrh and aloes and cassia;
from ivoried palaces
lutes entertain you.
10 Royal princesses are your favorites;
the consort stands at your right hand,
decked in gold of Ophir.

b-b Order of Heb clauses inverted for clarity

c-c Cf. I Chron. 29.23

11 Take heed, lass, and note,
incline your ear:
forget your people and your father's house,
12 and let the king be aroused by your beauty;
since he is your lord, bow to him.
13 O Tyrian lass,
the wealthiest people will court your favor with gifts,
14 [a-]goods of all sorts.
The royal princess,
her dress embroidered with golden mountings,
15 is led inside to the king;[-a]
maidens in her train, her companions,
are presented to you.
16 They are led in with joy and gladness;
they enter the palace of the king.
17 Your sons will succeed your ancestors;
you will appoint them princes throughout the land.

a-a Meaning of Heb uncertain

18 I commemorate your fame for all generations,
so peoples will praise you forever and ever.

46

For the leader.
[A psalm] of the Korahites.
[a-]On *alamoth*.[-a] A song.

a-a Meaning of Heb uncertain

2 God is our refuge and stronghold,
a help in trouble, very near.
3 Therefore we are not afraid

though the earth reels,
though mountains topple into the sea.
4 Its waters rage and foam;
in its swell mountains quake. *Selah*

5 There is a river whose streams gladden God's city,
the holy dwelling-place of the Most High.
6 God is in its midst, it will not be toppled;
by daybreak God will come to its aid.
7 Nations rage, kingdoms topple;
at the sound of His thunder the earth dissolves.
8 The LORD of hosts is with us;
the God of Jacob is our haven. *Selah*

9 Come and see what the LORD has done,
how He has wrought desolation on the earth.
10 He puts a stop to wars throughout the earth,
breaking the bow, snapping the spear,
consigning wagons to the flames.
11 "Desist! Realize that I am God!
I dominate the nations;
I dominate the earth."
12 The LORD of hosts is with us;
the God of Jacob is our haven. *Selah*

47

For the leader.
A psalm of the Korahites.

2 All you peoples, clap your hands,
raise a joyous shout for God.
3 For the LORD is most high, awesome,
great king over all the earth,
4 He subjects peoples to us,
sets nations at our feet.
5 He chose our heritage for us,
the pride of Jacob whom He loved. *Selah*

6 God ascends midst acclamation;
the LORD, to the blasts of the horn.
7 Sing, O sing to God;
sing, O sing to our king,
8 For God is king over all the earth;
sing a hymn.[a]
9 God reigns over the nations;
God is seated on His holy throne.

[a] *Heb* maskil, *a musical term of uncertain meaning*

10 The great of the peoples are gathered together,
the retinue of Abraham's God;
for the guardians of the earth belong to God;
He is greatly exalted.

48 A song, a psalm of the Korahites.

2 The LORD is great and much acclaimed
in the city of our God,
His holy mountain—
3 fair-crested, joy of all the earth,
Mount Zion, summit of Zaphon,[a]
city of the great king.
4 Through its citadels, God has made Himself known as a haven.
5 See, the kings joined forces;
they advanced together.
6 At the mere sight of it they were stunned,
they were terrified, they panicked,
7 they were seized there with a trembling,
like a woman in the throes of labor,
8 as the Tarshish fleet was wrecked
in an easterly gale.[b]
9 The likes of what we heard we have now witnessed
in the city of the LORD of hosts,
in the city of our God—
may God preserve it forever! *Selah*

10 In Your temple, God,
we meditate upon Your faithful care.
11 The praise of You, God, like Your name,
reaches to the ends of the earth;
Your right hand is filled with beneficence.
12 Let Mount Zion rejoice!
Let the towns[c] of Judah exult,
because of Your judgments.

13 Walk around Zion,
circle it;
count its towers,
14 take note of its rampart;
[d-]go through[-d] its citadels,
that you may recount it to a future age.
15 For God—He is our God forever;
He will lead us [d-]evermore.[-d]

[a] *A term for the divine abode*

[b] *See I Kings 22.49*

[c] *Or "women"*

[d-d] *Meaning of Heb uncertain*

49 For the leader.
A psalm of the Korahites.

2 Hear this, all you peoples;
give ear, all inhabitants of the world,
3 men of all estates,
rich and poor alike.
4 My mouth utters wisdom,
my thought is full of insight.
5 I will turn my attention to a theme,
set forth my lesson to the music of a lyre.

6 In time of trouble, why should I fear
the encompassing evil of my deceivers—
7 men who trust in their riches,
who glory in their great wealth?
8 [a-]Ah, it[-a] cannot redeem a man,
or pay his ransom to God;
9 the price of life is too high;
and so man ceases to be forever.
10 Shall he live eternally,
and never see the grave?
11 For one sees that the wise die,
that the foolish and ignorant both perish,
leaving their wealth to others.
12 Their grave[b] is their eternal home,
the dwelling-place for all generations
of those once famous on earth.
13 Man does not abide in honor;
he is like the beasts that perish.

14 Such is the fate of those who are self-confident,
[c-]the end of those pleased with their own speech.[-c] *Selah*
15 Sheeplike they head for Sheol,
with Death as their shepherd.
The upright shall rule over them at daybreak,
[c-]and their form shall waste away in Sheol
till its nobility be gone.[-c]
16 But God will redeem my life from the clutches of Sheol,
for He will take me. *Selah*

17 Do not be afraid when a man becomes rich,
when his household goods increase;
18 for when he dies he can take none of it along;

[a-a] Or "A brother"

[b] Taken with ancient versions and medieval commentators as the equivalent of qibram

[c-c] Meaning of Heb uncertain

his goods cannot follow him down.
19 Though he congratulates himself in his lifetime,
[c-]—"They must admit that you did well by yourself"—[-c]
20 yet he must join the company of his ancestors,
who will never see daylight again.
21 Man does not understand honor;
he is like the beasts that perish.

[c-c] *Meaning of Heb uncertain*

50 A psalm of Asaph.

[a-]God, the LORD God[-a] spoke
and summoned the world from east to west.
2 From Zion, perfect in beauty,
God appeared
3 —let our God come and not fail to act!
Devouring fire preceded Him;
it stormed around Him fiercely.
4 He summoned the heavens above,
and the earth, for the trial of His people.
5 "Bring in My devotees,
who made a covenant with Me over sacrifice!"
6 Then the heavens proclaimed His righteousness,
for He is a God who judges. *Selah*

[a-a] *Heb* 'El 'Elohim YHWH

7 "Pay heed, My people, and I will speak,
O Israel, and I will arraign you.
I am God, your God.
8 I censure you not for your sacrifices,
and your burnt offerings, made to Me daily;
9 I claim no bull from your estate,
no he-goats from your pens.
10 For Mine is every animal of the forest,
the beasts on [b-]a thousand mountains.[-b]
11 I know every bird of the mountains,
the creatures of the field are subject to Me.
12 Were I hungry, I would not tell you,
for Mine is the world and all it holds.
13 Do I eat the flesh of bulls,
or drink the blood of he-goats?
14 Sacrifice a thank offering to God,
and pay your vows to the Most High.
15 Call upon Me in time of trouble;
I will rescue you, and you shall honor Me."

[b-b] *Meaning of Heb uncertain*

16 And to the wicked, God said,
"Who are you to recite My laws,
and mouth the terms of My covenant,
17 seeing that you spurn My discipline,
and brush My words aside?
18 When you see a thief, you fall in with him,
and throw in your lot with adulterers;
19 you devote your mouth to evil,
and yoke your tongue to deceit;
20 you are busy maligning your brother,
defaming the son of your mother.
21 If I failed to act when you did these things,
you would fancy that I were like you;
so I censure you and confront you with charges.
22 Mark this, you who are unmindful of God,
lest I tear you apart and no one save you.

23 He who sacrifices a thank offering honors Me,
[b-]and to him who improves his way[-b]
I will show the salvation of God."

[b-b] *Meaning of Heb uncertain*

51

For the leader.
A psalm of David,
2 when Nathan the prophet came to him after
he had consorted with Bathsheba.[a]

[a] *Cf. II Sam. 12*

3 Have mercy upon me, O God,
as befits Your faithfulness;
in keeping with Your abundant compassion
blot out my transgressions.
4 Wash me thoroughly of my iniquity,
and purify me of my sin;
5 for I recognize my transgressions,
and am ever conscious of my sin;
6 against You alone have I sinned,
and done what is evil in Your sight;
so You are just in Your sentence,
and right in Your judgment.
7 Indeed I was born with iniquity;
with sin my mother conceived me.
8 [b-]Indeed You desire truth about that which is hidden;
teach me wisdom about secret things.[-b]

[b-b] *Meaning of Heb uncertain*

9 Purge me with hyssop till I am pure;
wash me till I am whiter than snow.
10 Let me hear tidings of joy and gladness;
let the bones You have crushed exult.
11 Hide Your face from my sins;
blot out all my iniquities.
12 Fashion a pure heart for me, O God;
create in me a steadfast spirit.
13 Do not cast me out of Your presence,
or take Your holy spirit away from me.
14 Let me again rejoice in Your help;
let a vigorous spirit sustain me.
15 Let me teach transgressors Your ways,
that sinners may return to You.

16 Save me from bloodguilt,
O God, God, my deliverer,
that I may sing forth Your beneficence.
17 O LORD, open my lips,
and let my mouth declare Your praise.
18 You do not want me to bring sacrifices;
You do not desire burnt offerings;
19 True sacrifice to God is a contrite spirit;
God, You will not despise
a contrite and crushed heart.

20 May it please You to make Zion prosper;
rebuild the walls of Jerusalem.
21 Then You will want sacrifices offered in righteousness,
burnt and whole offerings;
then bulls will be offered upon Your altar.

52

For the leader.
A *maskil* of David,
2 when Doeg the Edomite went and informed Saul, telling him, "David entered Ahimelech's sanctuary."[a]

[a] *Cf. I Sam. 22.9 f.*

3 Why do you boast of your evil, brave fellow?
God's faithfulness [b-]never ceases.[-b]
4 Your tongue devises mischief,
like a sharpened razor that works treacherously.
5 You prefer evil to good,
the lie, to speaking truthfully. *Selah*

[b-b] *Lit. "is all the day"*

6 You love all pernicious words,
treacherous speech.
7 So God will tear you down for good,
will break you and pluck you from your tent,
and root you out of the land of the living. *Selah*
8 The righteous, seeing it, will be awestruck;
they will jibe at him, saying,
9 "Here was a fellow who did not make God his refuge,
but trusted in his great wealth,
relied upon his mischief."

10 But I am like a thriving olive tree in God's house;
I trust in the faithfulness of God forever and ever.
11 I praise You forever, for You have acted;
[c]I declare that Your name is good[-c]
in the presence of Your faithful ones.

c-c Meaning of Heb uncertain; others "I will wait for Your name for it is good"

53[a]

For the leader; on *mahalath*.[b]
A *maskil* of David.

a Cf. Psalm 14
b Meaning of Heb unknown

2 The benighted man thinks,
[c]"God does not care."[-c]
Man's wrongdoing is corrupt and loathsome;
no one does good.
3 The LORD looks down from heaven on mankind
to find a man of understanding,
a man mindful of God.
4 Everyone is dross,
altogether foul;
there is none who does good,
not even one.
5 Are they so witless, those evildoers,
who devour my people as they devour food,
and do not invoke God?
6 There they will be seized with fright
—[d]never was there such a fright—
for God has scattered the bones of your besiegers;
you have put them to shame,[-d]
for God has rejected them.

7 O that the deliverance of Israel might come from Zion!
When God restores the fortunes of His people,
Jacob will exult, Israel will rejoice.

c-c Lit. "There is no God"
d-d Meaning of Heb uncertain

54 For the leader; with instrumental music.
A *maskil* of David,

2 when the Ziphites came and told Saul, "You must know, David is in hiding among us."[a]

[a] *Cf. I Sam. 23.19*

3 O God, deliver me by Your name;
by Your power vindicate me.
4 O God, hear my prayer;
give ear to the words of my mouth.
5 For strangers have risen against me,
and ruthless men seek my life;
they are unmindful of God. *Selah*

6 See, God is my helper;
the LORD is my support.
7 He will repay the evil of my watchful foes;
by Your faithfulness, destroy them!
8 Then I will offer You a free-will sacrifice;
I will acknowledge that Your name, LORD, is good,
9 for it has saved me from my foes,
and let me gaze triumphant upon my enemies.

55 For the leader; with instrumental music.
A *maskil* of David.

2 Give ear, O God, to my prayer;
do not ignore my plea;
3 pay heed to me and answer me.
I am tossed about, complaining and moaning
4 at the clamor of the enemy,
because of the oppression of the wicked;
for they bring evil upon me
and angrily harass me.
5 My heart is convulsed within me;
terrors of death assail me.
6 Fear and trembling invade me;
I am clothed with horror.
7 I said:
"O that I had the wings of a dove!
I would fly away and find rest;
8 lo, I would flee far off;
I would lodge in the wilderness; *Selah*

9 I would soon find me a refuge
from the sweeping wind,
from the tempest."

10 O LORD, confound their speech, confuse it!
For I see lawlessness and strife in the city;
11 day and night they make their rounds on its walls;
evil and mischief are inside it.
12 Malice is within it;
fraud and deceit never leave its square.

13 It is not an enemy who reviles me
—I could bear that;
it is not my foe who vaunts himself against me
—I could hide from him;
14 but it is you, my equal,
my companion, my friend;
15 sweet was our fellowship;
we walked together in God's house.
16 Let Him incite death against them;
may they go down alive into Sheol!
For where they dwell,
there evil is.

17 As for me, I call to God;
the LORD will deliver me.
18 Evening, morning, and noon
I complain and moan,
and He hears my voice.
19 He redeems me unharmed
from the battle against me;
[a-]it is as though many are on my side.[-a]
20 God who has reigned from the first,
who will have no successor,
hears and humbles them who have no fear of God. *Selah*

21 He[b] harmed his ally,
he broke his pact;
22 his talk was smoother than butter,
yet his mind was on war;
his words were more soothing than oil,
yet they were drawn swords.

23 Cast your burden on the LORD and He will sustain you;
He will never let the righteous man collapse.

[a-a] Meaning of Heb uncertain

[b] I.e. the friend of v. 14

24 For You, O God, will bring them down to the nethermost pit—
those murderous, treacherous men;
they shall not live out half their days;
but I trust in You.

56

For the leader; [a]on *jonath-elem-rehokim.*[-a]
A *michtam* of David,
when the Philistines seized him in Gath.

[a-a] *Meaning of Heb uncertain*

2 Have mercy on me, O God,
for men persecute me;
all day long my adversary oppresses me.
3 My watchful foes persecute me all day long;
many are my adversaries, O Exalted One.
4 When I am afraid, I trust in You,
5 in God, whose word I praise;
in God I trust;
I am not afraid;
what can mortals[b] do to me?
6 All day long [a]they cause me grief in my affairs,[-a]
they plan only evil against me.
7 They are stirred up, they lie in ambush;
they watch my every move, hoping for my death.
8 Cast them out for their evil;
subdue peoples in Your anger, O God.

[b] *Lit. "flesh"*

9 [a]You keep count of my wanderings;
put my tears into Your flask,
into Your record.[-a]
10 Then my enemies will retreat when I call on You;
this I know, that God is for me.
11 In God, whose word I praise,
in the LORD, whose word I praise,
12 in God I trust;
I am not afraid;
what can man do to me?
13 I must pay my vows to You, O God;
I will render thank-offerings to You.
14 For You have saved me from death,
my foot from stumbling,
that I may walk before God in the light of life.

57

For the leader; [a]*al-tashheth.*[a]
A *michtam* of David,
when he fled from Saul into a cave.

[a-a] *Meaning of Heb uncertain*

2 Have pity on me, O God, have pity on me,
for I seek refuge in You,
I seek refuge in the shadow of Your wings,
until danger passes.
3 I call to God, most high,
to God who is good to me.
4 He will reach down from heaven and deliver me:
God will send down His steadfast love;
my persecutor reviles. *Selah*

5 As for me, I lie down among man-eating lions
whose teeth are spears and arrows,
whose tongue is a sharp sword.
6 Exalt Yourself over the heavens, O God,
let Your glory be over all the earth!
7 They prepared a net for my feet [b]to ensnare me;[b]
they dug a pit for me,
but they fell into it. *Selah*

[b-b] *Cf. Mishnaic Heb* kefifah, *a wicker basket used in fishing*

8[c] My heart is firm, O God;
my heart is firm;
I will sing, I will chant a hymn.
9 Awake, O my soul!
Awake, O harp and lyre!
I will wake the dawn.
10 I will praise You among the peoples, O LORD;
I will sing a hymn to You among the nations;
11 for Your faithfulness is as high as heaven;
Your steadfastness reaches to the sky.
12 Exalt Yourself over the heavens, O God,
let Your glory be over all the earth!

[c] *With vv. 8–12, cf. Ps. 108.2–6*

58

For the leader; *al-tashheth:*
A *michtam* of David.

2 [a]O mighty ones,[a] do you really decree what is just?
Do you judge mankind with equity?
3 In your minds you devise wrongdoing in the land;
[a]with your hands you deal out lawlessness.[a]

[a-a] *Meaning of Heb uncertain*

4 The wicked are defiant from birth;
the liars go astray from the womb.
5 Their venom is like that of a snake,
a deaf viper that stops its ears
6 so as not to hear the voice of charmers
or the expert mutterer of spells.

7 O God, smash their teeth in their mouth;
shatter the fangs of lions, O LORD;
8 let them melt, let them vanish like water;
let Him aim His arrows and they be cut down;
9 [a]-like a snail that melts away as it moves;-[a]
like a woman's stillbirth, may they never see the sun!
10 Before [a]-the thorns grow into a bramble,
may He whirl them away alive in fury.-[a]

[a-a] *Meaning of Heb uncertain*

11 The righteous man will rejoice when he sees revenge;
he will bathe his feet in the blood of the wicked.
12 Men will say:
"There is, then, a reward for the righteous;
indeed, God does judge on earth."

59

For the leader; *al-tashheth.*
A *michtam* of David,
when Saul sent men to watch his house in order to put him to death.[a]

[a] *Cf. I Sam. 19.11*

2 Save me from my enemies, O my God;
secure me against my assailants.
3 Save me from evildoers;
deliver me from murderers.
4 For see, they lie in wait for me;
fierce men are stirred up against me
for no offense of mine,
for no transgression, O LORD;
5 for no guilt of mine
do they rush to array themselves against me.
Look, rouse Yourself on my behalf!
6 You, O LORD God of hosts,
God of Israel,
bestir Yourself to bring all nations to account;
have no pity on all the treacherous villains. *Selah*

7 They come each evening growling like dogs,
roaming the city.

8 They rave with their mouths,
[b]sharp words[b] are on their lips,
[they think,] "Who hears?"
9 But You, O LORD, laugh at them;
You mock all the nations.

[b-b] *Lit. "swords"*

10 O my[c] strength, I wait for You;
for God is my haven.
11 My faithful God will come to aid me;
God will let me gloat over my watchful foes.
12 Do not kill them lest my people be unmindful;
with Your power make wanderers of them;
bring them low, O our shield, the Lord,
13 because of their sinful mouths,
the words on their lips.
Let them be trapped by their pride,
and by the imprecations and lies they utter.
14 In Your fury put an end to them;
put an end to them that they be no more;
that it may be known to the ends of the earth
that God does rule over Jacob. *Selah*

[c] *With several mss.; cf. v. 18; lit. "His"*

15 They come each evening growling like dogs,
roaming the city.
16 They wander in search of food;
and whine if they are not satisfied.
17 But I will sing of Your strength,
extol each morning Your faithfulness;
for You have been my haven,
a refuge in time of trouble.

18 O my strength, to You I sing hymns;
for God is my haven, my faithful God.

60

For the leader; on [a]*shushan eduth.*[a]
A *michtam* of David (to be taught),
2 when he fought with Aram Naharaim and
Aram-Zobah, and Joab came back and inflicted
twelve thousand casualties on Edom in the
Valley of Salt.[b]

[a-a] *Meaning of Heb uncertain*

[b] *Cf. II Sam. 8; I Chron. 18*

3 O God, You have rejected us,
You have made a breach in us;
You have been angry;
restore us!

4 You have made the land quake;
You have torn it open.
Mend its fissures,
for it is collapsing.
5 You have made Your people suffer hardship;
[c]You have given us wine that makes us reel.[c]
6 [a]Give those who fear You because of Your truth
a banner for rallying.[a] *Selah*
7[d] That those whom You love might be rescued,
deliver with Your right hand and answer me.

[c-c] Or "You have sated Your people with a bitter draught"

[a-a] Meaning of Heb uncertain

[d] Cf. Ps. 108.7–14

8 God promised [e]in His sanctuary[e]
that I would exultingly divide up Shechem,
and measure the Valley of Sukkoth;
9 Gilead and Manasseh would be mine,
Ephraim my chief stronghold,
Judah my scepter;
10 Moab would be my wash-basin;
on Edom I would cast my shoe;
acclaim me, O Philistia!

[e-e] Or "by His holiness"

11 Would that I were brought to the bastion!
Would that I were led to Edom!

12 But You have rejected us, O God;
God, You do not march with our armies.
13 Grant us Your aid against the foe,
for the help of man is worthless.
14 With God we shall triumph;
He will trample our foes.

61

For the leader; with instrumental music.
[A psalm] of David.

2 Hear my cry, O God,
heed my prayer.
3 From the end of the earth I call to You;
when my heart is faint,
You lead me to a rock that is high above me.
4 For You have been my refuge,
a tower of strength against the enemy.
5 O that I might dwell in Your tent forever,
take refuge under Your protecting wings. *Selah*

6 O God, You have heard my vows;
grant the request of those who fear Your name.

7 Add days to the days of the king;
may his years extend through generations;
8 may he dwell in God's presence forever;
appoint[a] steadfast love to guard him.

[a] *Meaning of Heb uncertain*

9 So I will sing hymns to Your name forever,
as I fulfill my vows day after day.

62

For the leader; for Jeduthun.
[A psalm] of David.

2 Truly my soul waits quietly for God;
my deliverance comes from Him.
3 Truly He is my rock and deliverance,
my haven; I shall never be shaken.
4 How long will all of you attack[a] a man,
to crush[a] him, as though he were
a leaning wall, a tottering fence?

[a] *Meaning of Heb uncertain*

5 They lay plans to topple him from his rank;
they delight in falsehood;
they bless with their mouths,
while inwardly they curse. *Selah*

6 Truly, wait quietly for God, O my soul,
for my hope comes from Him.
7 He is my rock and deliverance,
my haven; I shall not be shaken.
8 I rely on God, my deliverance and glory,
my rock of strength;
in God is my refuge.
9 Trust in Him at all times, O people;
pour out your heart before Him;
God is our refuge. *Selah*

10 Men are mere breath;
mortals, illusion;
placed on a scale all together,
they weigh even less than a breath.
11 Do not trust in violence,
or put false hopes in robbery;
if force bears fruit pay it no mind.
12 One thing God has spoken;
two things have I heard:
that might belongs to God,
13 and faithfulness is Yours, O Lord,
to reward each man according to his deeds.

63 A psalm of David,
when he was in the Wilderness of Judah.

2 God, You are my God;
I search for You,
my soul thirsts for You,
my body yearns for You,
as a parched and thirsty land that has no water.
3 I shall behold You in the sanctuary,
and see Your might and glory,
4 Truly Your faithfulness is better than life;
my lips declare Your praise.
5 I bless You all my life;
I lift up my hands, invoking Your name.
6 I am sated as with a [a]rich feast,[a]
I sing praises with joyful lips,
7 when I call You to mind upon my bed,
when I think of You in the watches of the night;
8 for You are my help,
and in the shadow of Your wings
I shout for joy.
9 My soul is attached to You;
Your right hand supports me.

10 May those who seek to destroy my life
enter the depths of the earth.
11 May they be gutted by the sword;
may they be prey to foxes.
12 But the king shall rejoice in God;
all who swear by Him shall exult,
when the mouth of liars is stopped.

a-a *Lit. "suet and fat"*

64 For the leader.
A psalm of David.

2 Hear my voice, O God, when I plead;
guard my life from the enemy's terror.
3 Hide me from a band of evil men,
from a crowd of evildoers,
4 who whet their tongues like swords;
they aim their arrows—cruel words—
5 to shoot from hiding at the blameless;
they shoot him suddenly and without fear.

6 [a-]They arm themselves with an evil word;
when they speak, it is to conceal traps;[-a]
they think: "Who will see them?"
7[b] Let the wrongdoings they have concealed,[c]
each one inside him, his secret thoughts,
be wholly exposed.
8 God shall shoot them with arrows;
they shall be struck down suddenly.
9 Their tongue shall be their downfall;
all who see them shall recoil in horror;
10 all men shall stand in awe;
they shall proclaim the work of God
and His deed which they perceived.
11 The righteous shall rejoice in the LORD,
and take refuge in Him;
all the upright shall exult.

[a-a] *Meaning of Heb uncertain*

[b] *Meaning of verse uncertain*

[c] *Reading* tamnu *with some mss.* (*cf.* Minhat Shai) *and Rashi; most printed editions,* tamnu, *traditionally rendered "they have accomplished"*

65

For the leader.
A psalm, a song of David.

2 Praise befits You in Zion, O God;
vows are paid to You;
all mankind[a] comes to You,
3 You who hears prayer.
4 When all manner of sins overwhelm me,
it is You who forgives our iniquities.
5 Happy is the man You choose and bring near
to dwell in Your courts;
may we be sated with the blessings of Your house,
Your holy temple.

6 Answer us with victory through awesome deeds,
O God, our deliverer,
in whom all the ends of the earth
and the distant seas
put their trust;
7 who by His power fixed the mountains firmly,
who is girded with might,
8 who stills the raging seas,
the raging waves
and tumultuous peoples.
9 Those who live at the ends of the earth are awed by Your signs;
You make the lands of sunrise and sunset shout for joy.

[a] *Lit. "flesh"*

10 You take care of the earth and irrigate it;
You enrich it greatly,
with the channel of God full of water;
You provide grain for men;
for so do You prepare it.
11 Saturating its furrows,
leveling its ridges,
You soften it with showers,
You bless its growth.
12 You crown the year with Your bounty;
fatness is distilled in Your paths;
13 the pasture lands distill it;
the hills are girded with joy.
14 The meadows are clothed with flocks,
the valleys mantled with grain;
they raise a shout, they break into song.

66

For the leader.
A song, a psalm.

2 Raise a shout for God, all the earth;
sing the glory of His name,
make glorious His praise.
3 Say to God:
"How awesome are Your deeds,
Your enemies cower before Your great strength;
4 all the earth bows to You,
and sings hymns to You;
all sing hymns to Your name." *Selah*

5 Come and see the works of God
who is held in awe by men for His acts.
6 He turned the sea into dry land;
they crossed the river on foot;
we therefore rejoice in Him.
7 He rules forever in His might;
His eyes scan the nations;
let not the rebellious assert themselves. *Selah*

8 O peoples, bless our God,
celebrate His praises;
9 who has granted us life,
and has not let our feet slip.

10 You have tried us, O God,
refining us, as one refines silver.
11 You have caught us in a net,
[a]caught us in trammels.[a]
12 You have let men ride over us;
we have endured fire and water,
and You have brought us through to prosperity.

13 I enter Your house with burnt offerings,
I pay my vows to You,
14 [vows] that my lips pronounced,
that my mouth uttered in my distress.
15 I offer up fatlings to You,
with the odor of burning rams;
I sacrifice bulls and he-goats. *Selah*

16 Come and hear, all God-fearing men,
as I tell what He did for me.
17 I called aloud to Him,
glorification on my tongue.
18 Had I an evil thought in my mind,
the LORD would not have listened.
19 But God did listen,
He paid heed to my prayer.
20 Blessed is God who has not turned away my prayer,
or His faithful care from me.

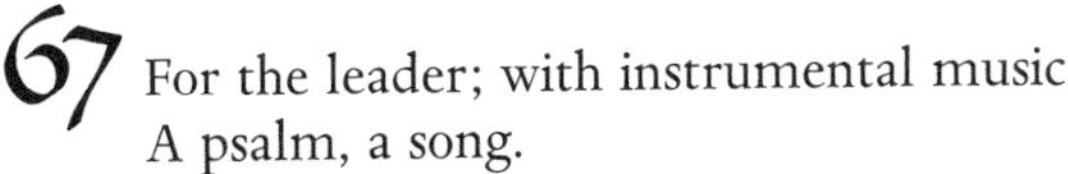

67 For the leader; with instrumental music. A psalm, a song.

2 May God be gracious to us and bless us;
may He show us favor, *Selah*
3 that Your way be known on earth,
Your deliverance among all nations.

4 Peoples will praise You, O God;
all peoples will praise You.
5 Nations will exult and shout for joy,
for You rule the peoples with equity,
guide the nations of the earth. *Selah*
6 The peoples will praise You, O God;
all peoples will praise You.

[a-a] Lit. "put a trammel on our loins"

7 May the earth yield its produce;
may God, our God, bless us.
8 May God bless us,
and be revered to the ends of the earth.

68[a]

For the leader.
A psalm, a song of David.

[a] *The coherence of this psalm and the meaning of many of its passages are uncertain*

2 God will arise,
His enemies shall be scattered,
His foes shall flee before Him.
3 Disperse them as smoke is dispersed;
as wax melts at fire,
so the wicked shall perish before God.
4 But the righteous shall rejoice;
they shall exult in the presence of God;
they shall be exceedingly joyful.

5 Sing to God, chant hymns to His name;
extol Him who rides the clouds;
the LORD is His name.
Exult in His presence—
6 the father of orphans, the champion of widows,
God, in His holy habitation.
7 God restores the lonely to their homes,
sets free the imprisoned, safe and sound,
while the rebellious must live in a parched land.

8 O God, when You went at the head of Your army,
when You marched through the desert, *Selah*
9 the earth trembled, the sky rained because of God,
yon Sinai, because of God, the God of Israel.
10 You released a bountiful rain, O God;
when Your own land languished, You sustained it.
11 Your tribe dwells there;
O God, in Your goodness You provide for the needy.

12 The LORD gives a command;
the women who bring the news are a great host:
13 "The kings and their armies are in headlong flight;
housewives are sharing in the spoils;
14 even for those of you who lie among the sheepfolds
there are wings of a dove sheathed in silver,
its pinions in fine gold."

15 When Shaddai scattered the kings,
it seemed like a snowstorm in Zalmon.

16 O majestic mountain, Mount Bashan;
O jagged mountain, Mount Bashan;
17 why so hostile, O jagged mountains,
toward the mountain God desired as His dwelling?
The Lord shall abide there forever.

18 God's chariots are myriads upon myriads,
thousands upon thousands;
the Lord is among them as in Sinai in holiness.

19 You went up to the heights, having taken captives,
having received tribute of men,
even of those who rebel
against the LORD God's abiding there.

20 Blessed is the LORD.
Day by day He supports us,
God, our deliverance. *Selah*
21 God is for us a God of deliverance;
GOD the LORD provides an escape from death.
22 God will smash the heads of His enemies,
the hairy crown of him who walks about in his guilt.
23 The LORD said, "I will retrieve from Bashan,
I will retrieve from the depths of the sea;
24 that your feet may wade through blood;
that the tongue of your dogs may have its portion of your enemies."

25 Men see Your processions, O God,
the processions of my God, my king,
into the sanctuary.
26 First come singers, then musicians,
amidst maidens playing timbrels.
27 In assemblies bless God,
the LORD, O you who are from the fountain of Israel.
28 There is little Benjamin who rules them,
the princes of Judah who command them,
the princes of Zebulon and Naphtali.

29 Your God has ordained strength for you,
the strength, O God,
which You displayed for us
30 from Your temple above Jerusalem.
The kings bring You tribute.

31 Blast the beast of the marsh,
the herd of bulls among the peoples, the calves,
till they come cringing with pieces of silver.
Scatter the peoples who delight in wars!
32 Tribute-bearers shall come from Egypt;
Cush shall hasten its gifts to God.

33 O kingdoms of the earth,
sing to God;
chant hymns to the Lord, *Selah*
34 to Him who rides the ancient highest heavens,
who thunders forth with His mighty voice.
35 Ascribe might to God
whose majesty is over Israel,
whose might is in the skies.
36 You are awesome, O God, in Your holy places;
it is the God of Israel who gives might and power to the people.
Blessed is God.

69

For the leader; on *shoshannim*.[a]
[A psalm] of David.

[a] *Meaning of Heb uncertain*

2 Deliver me, O God,
for the waters have reached my neck;
3 I am sinking into the slimy deep
and find no foothold;
I have come into the watery depths;
the flood sweeps me away.
4 I am weary with calling;
my throat is dry;
my eyes fail
while I wait for God.
5 More numerous than the hairs of my head
are those who hate me without reason;
many are those who would destroy me,
my enemies without cause.
Must I restore what I have not stolen?

6 God, You know my folly;
my guilty deeds are not hidden from You.
7 Let those who look to You,
O Lord, God of hosts,
not be disappointed on my account;
let those who seek You,

O God of Israel,
not be shamed because of me.
8 It is for Your sake that I have been reviled,
that shame covers my face;
9 I am a stranger to my brothers,
an alien to my kin.
10 My zeal for Your house has been my undoing;
the reproaches of those who revile You have fallen upon me.
11 When I wept and fasted,
I was reviled for it.
12 I made sackcloth my garment;
I became a byword among them.
13 Those who sit in the gate talk about me;
I am the taunt of drunkards.

14 As for me, may my prayer come to You, O LORD,
at a favorable moment;
O God, in Your abundant faithfulness,
answer me with Your sure deliverance.
15 Rescue me from the mire;
let me not sink;
let me be rescued from my enemies,
and from the watery depths.
16 Let the floodwaters not sweep me away;
let the deep not swallow me;
let the mouth of the well not close over me.
17 Answer me, O LORD,
according to Your great steadfastness;
in accordance with Your abundant mercy
turn to me,
18 do not hide Your face from Your servant,
for I am in distress;
answer me quickly.
19 Come near to me and redeem me;
free me from my enemies.

20 You know my reproach,
my shame, my disgrace;
You are aware of all my foes.
21 Reproach breaks my heart,
I am in despair;[a]
I hope for consolation, but there is none,
for comforters, but find none.
22 They give me gall for food,
vinegar to quench my thirst.

[a] *Meaning of Heb uncertain*

23 May their table be a trap for them,
a snare for their allies.
24 May their eyes grow dim so that they cannot see;
may their loins collapse continually.
25 Pour out Your wrath on them;
may Your blazing anger overtake them;
26 may their encampments be desolate;
may their tents stand empty.
27 For they persecute those You have struck;
they talk about the pain of those You have felled.
28 Add this to their guilt;
let them have no share of Your beneficence.
29 May they be erased from the book of life,
and not be inscribed with the righteous.

30 But I am lowly and in pain;
Your help, O God, keeps me safe.
31 I will extol God's name with song,
and exalt Him with praise.
32 That will please the LORD more than oxen,
than bulls with horns and hooves.
33 The lowly will see and rejoice;
you who are mindful of God, take heart!
34 For the LORD listens to the needy,
and does not spurn His captives.

35 Heaven and earth shall extol Him,
the seas, and all that moves in them.
36 For God will deliver Zion
and rebuild the cities of Judah;
they shall live there and inherit it;
37 the offspring of His servants shall possess it;
those who cherish His name shall dwell there.

70

For the leader.
[A psalm] of David.
Lehazkir.

2 [a]Hasten, O God, to save me;
O LORD, to aid me!
3 Let those who seek my life
be frustrated and disgraced;
let those who wish me harm,
fall back in shame.
4 Let those who say, "Aha! Aha!"

[a] *Cf.* 40.14–18

turn back because of their frustration.

5 But let all who seek You be glad and rejoice in You;
let those who are eager for Your deliverance always say,
"Extolled be God!"
6 But I am poor and needy;
O God, hasten to me!
You are my help and my rescuer;
O LORD, do not delay.

71

I seek refuge in You, O LORD;
may I never be disappointed.
2 As You are beneficent, save me and rescue me;
incline Your ear to me and deliver me.
3 Be a sheltering rock for me to which I may always repair;
decree my deliverance,
for You are my rock and my fortress.
4 My God, rescue me from the hand of the wicked,
from the grasp of the unjust and the lawless,

5 For You my Lord are my hope;
O God, You are my trust from my youth.
6 While yet unborn, I depended on You;
in the womb of my mother, You were my support;[a]
I sing Your praises always.
7 I have become an example for many,
since You are my mighty refuge.
8 My mouth is full of praise to You,
glorifying You all day long.
9 Do not cast me off in old age;
when my strength fails, do not forsake me!

10 For my enemies talk against me;
those who wait for me are of one mind,
11 Saying, "God has forsaken him;
chase him and catch him,
for no one will save him!"
12 O God, be not far from me;
my God, hasten to my aid!
13 Let my accusers perish in frustration;
let those who seek my ruin be clothed in reproach and disgrace!

14 As for me, I will hope always,
and add to the many praises of You.
15 My mouth tells of Your beneficence,

[a] *Meaning of Heb uncertain*

of Your deliverance all day long,
though I know not how to tell it.
16 [b-]I come with praise of Your mighty acts, O Lord GOD;
I celebrate[-b] Your beneficence, Yours alone.
17 You have let me experience it, God, from my youth;
until now I have proclaimed Your wondrous deeds,
18 and even in hoary old age do not forsake me, God,
until I proclaim Your strength to the next generation,
19 Your mighty acts, to all who are to come,
Your beneficence, high as the heavens, O God,
you who have done great things;
O God, who is Your peer!
20 You who have made me undergo many troubles and misfortunes
will revive me again,
and raise me up from the depths of the earth.
21 You will grant me much greatness,
You will turn and comfort me.
22 Then I will acclaim You to the music of the lyre
for Your faithfulness, O my God;
I will sing a hymn to You with a harp,
O Holy One of Israel.
23 My lips shall be jubilant, as I sing a hymn to You,
my whole being, which You have redeemed.
24 All day long my tongue shall recite Your beneficent acts,
how those who sought my ruin were frustrated and disgraced.

b-b Or "Let me reach old age, O Lord GOD, celebrating"

72 [A psalm] of Solomon.

O God, endow the king with Your judgments,
the king's son with Your righteousness;
2 that he judge Your people rightly;
Your lowly ones, justly.
3 Let the mountains produce well-being for the people;
the hills, the reward of justice.
4 Let him champion the lowly among the people,
deliver the needy folk,
and crush those who wrong them.
5 Let them fear You as long as the sun shines,
while the moon lasts, generations on end.
6 Let him be like rain that falls on a mown field,
like a downpour of rain on the ground,
7 that the righteous may flourish in his time,
and well-being abound, till the moon is no more.
8 Let him rule from sea to sea,

from the river to the ends of the earth.
9 Let desert-dwellers kneel before him,
and his enemies lick the dust;
10 let kings of Tarshish and the islands pay tribute,
kings of Sheba and Seba offer gifts.
11 Let all kings bow to him,
and all nations serve him.

12 For he saves the needy who cry out,
the lowly who have no helper.
13 He cares about the wretched needy;
He brings the needy deliverance.
14 He redeems them from fraud and lawlessness;
[a-]the shedding of their blood weighs heavily upon him.[-a]

15 So let him live, and receive gold of Sheba;
let prayers for him be said always,
blessings on him invoked at all times.
16 [b-]Let abundant grain be in the land, to the tops of the mountains;
let his crops thrive like the forest of Lebanon;
and let men sprout up in towns like country grass.
17 May his name be eternal;
while the sun lasts, may his name endure;[-b]
let men invoke his blessedness upon themselves:
let all nations count him happy.

18 Blessed is the LORD God, God of Israel,
who alone does wondrous things;
19 Blessed is His glorious name forever,
and let His glory fill the whole world;
Amen and Amen.

20 End of the prayers of David son of Jesse.

[a-a] Or "their life is precious in his sight"

[b-b] Meaning of some Heb phrases in these verses uncertain

BOOK THREE

73 A psalm of Asaph.

God is truly good to Israel,
to those whose heart is pure.
2 As for me, my feet had almost strayed,
my steps were nearly led off course,

3 for I envied the profligate,
I saw the wicked at ease.
4 Death has no pangs for them;
their body is healthy.
5 They have no part in the travail of men;
they are not afflicted like the rest of mankind.
6 So pride adorns their necks,
lawlessness enwraps them as a mantle.
7 [a]Fat shuts out their eyes;
their fancies are extravagant.[a]
8 They scoff and plan evil;
from their eminence they plan wrongdoing.
9 They set their mouths against heaven,.
and their tongues range over the earth.
10 [a]So they pound His people again and again,
until they are drained of their very last tear.[a]
11 Then they say, "How could God know?
Is there knowledge with the Most High?"
12 Such are the wicked;
ever tranquil, they amass wealth.

13 It was for nothing that I kept my heart pure
and washed my hands in innocence,
14 seeing that I have been constantly afflicted,
that each morning brings new punishments.
15 Had I decided to say these things,
I should have been false to the circle of Your disciples.
16 So I applied myself to understand this,
but it seemed a hopeless task
17 till I entered God's sanctuary
and reflected on their fate.

18 You surround them with flattery,
make them fall through blandishments.
19 How suddenly are they ruined,
wholly swept away by terrors.
20 [a]When You are aroused You despise their image,
as one does a dream after waking, O LORD.[a]

21 My mind was stripped of its reason,
[b]my feelings were numbed.[b]
22 I was a dolt, without knowledge;
I was brutish toward You.

23 Yet I was always with You,

[a-a] Meaning of Heb uncertain

[b-b] Lit. "I was pierced through in my kidneys"

You held my right hand;
24 You guided me by Your counsel
[c-]and led me toward honor.[-c]
25 Whom else have I in heaven?
And having You, I want no one on earth.
26 My body and mind fail;
but God is the stay[d] of my mind, my portion forever.
27 Those who keep far from You perish;
You annihilate all who are untrue to You.
28 As for me, nearness to God is good;
I have made the Lord God my refuge
that I may recount all Your works.

[c-c] *Meaning of Heb uncertain; others "And afterward receive me with glory"*

[d] *Lit. "rock"*

74

A *maskil* of Asaph.

Why, O God, do You forever reject us,
do You fume in anger at the flock that You tend?
2 Remember the community You made Yours long ago,
You redeemed Your very own tribe;
[remember] Mount Zion, where You dwell.
3 [a-]Bestir Yourself[-a] because of the [b-]perpetual tumult,[-b]
all the outrages of the enemy in the sanctuary.
4 Your foes roar inside Your meeting-place;
they take their signs for true signs.
5 [b-]It is like men wielding axes
against a gnarled tree;
6 with hatchet and pike
they hacked away at its carved work.[-b]
7 They made Your sanctuary go up in flames;
they brought low in dishonor the dwelling-place of Your presence.
8 They resolved, "Let us destroy them altogether!"
They burned all God's tabernacles in the land.
9 No signs appear for us;
there is no longer any prophet;
no one among us knows for how long.

10 Till when, O God, will the foe blaspheme,
will the enemy forever revile Your name?
11 Why do You hold back Your hand, Your right hand?
[b-]Draw it out of Your bosom![-b]

12 O God, my king from of old,
who brings deliverance throughout the land;
13 it was You who drove back the sea with Your might,

[a-a] *Lit. "Lift up Your feet"*

[b-b] *Meaning of Heb uncertain*

who smashed the heads of the monsters in the waters;
14 it was You who crushed the heads of Leviathan,
who left him as food for [c]the denizens of the desert;[c]
15 it was You who released springs and torrents,
who made mighty rivers run dry;
16 the day is Yours, the night also;
it was You who set in place the orb of the sun;
17 You fixed all the boundaries of the earth;
summer and winter—You made them.

[c-c] *Or "seafaring men"; meaning of Heb uncertain*

18 Be mindful of how the enemy blasphemes the LORD,
how base people revile Your name.
19 Do not deliver Your dove to the wild beast;
do not ignore forever the band of Your lowly ones.
20 Look to the covenant!
For the dark places of the land are full of the haunts of lawlessness.
21 Let not the downtrodden turn away disappointed;
let the poor and needy praise Your name.
22 Rise, O God, champion Your cause;
be mindful that You are blasphemed by base men all day.
23 Do not ignore the shouts of Your foes,
the din of Your adversaries that rises all the time.

75

For the leader; *al-tashheth.*
A psalm of Asaph, a song.

2 We praise You, O God;
we praise You;
your presence[a] is near;
men tell of Your wondrous deeds.

[a] *Lit. "name"*

3 "At the time I choose,
I will give judgment equitably.
4 Earth and all its inhabitants dissolve;
it is I who keep its pillars firm. *Selah*
5 To wanton men I say, 'Do not be wanton!'
to the wicked, 'Do not lift up your horns!' "

6 Do not lift your horns up high
[b]in vainglorious bluster.[b]
7 For what lifts a man comes not from the east
or the west or the wilderness;
8 for God it is who gives judgment;
one man He brings down, another He lifts up.

[b] *Lit. "with the neck"*

9 There is a cup in God's hand
with foaming wine fully mixed;
from this He pours;
all the wicked of the earth drink,
draining it to the very dregs.
10 As for me, I will tell this forever;
I will sing a hymn to the God of Jacob.

11 "All the horns of the wicked I will cut;
but the horns of the righteous shall be lifted up."

76

For the leader; with instrumental music.
A psalm of Asaph, a song.

2 God has made Himself known in Judah,
His name is great in Israel;
3 Salem became His abode;
Zion, His den.
4 There He broke the fiery arrows of the bow,
the shield and the sword of war. *Selah*

5 You were resplendent,
glorious, on the mountains of prey.
6 The stout-hearted were despoiled;
they were in a stupor;
the bravest of men could not lift a hand.
7 At Your blast, O God of Jacob,
horse and chariot lay stunned.
8 O You! You are awesome!
Who can withstand You
when You are enraged?
9 In heaven You pronounced sentence;
the earth was numbed with fright
10 as God rose to execute judgment,
to deliver all the lowly of the earth. *Selah*

11 [a]-The fiercest of men shall acknowledge You,
when You gird on the last bit of fury.-[a]
12 Make vows and pay them to the LORD your God;
[a]-all who are around Him shall bring tribute to
the Awesome One.-[a]
13 He curbs the spirit of princes,
inspires awe in the kings of the earth.

[a-a] *Meaning of Heb uncertain*

77 For the leader; for Jeduthun.
A psalm of Asaph.

2 I cry aloud to God;
I cry to God that He give ear to me.
3 In my time of distress I turn to the Lord,
[a]with my hand [uplifted];
[my eyes] flow all night without respite;[a]
I will not be comforted.
4 I call God to mind, I moan,
I complain, my spirit fails. *Selah*

5 You have held my eyelids open;
I am overwrought, I cannot speak.
6 My thoughts turn to days of old,
to years long past.
7 I recall at night their jibes at me;
I commune with myself;
my spirit enquires,
8 "Will the Lord reject forever
and never again show favor?
9 Has His faithfulness disappeared forever?
Will His promise be unfulfilled for all time?
10 Has God forgotten how to pity?
Has He in anger stifled His compassion?" *Selah*
11 And I said, [a]"It is my fault
that the right hand of the Most High has changed."[a]

12 I recall the deeds of the LORD;
yes, I recall Your wonders of old;
13 I recount all Your works;
I speak of Your acts.
14 O God, Your ways are holiness;
what god is as great as God?
15 You are the God who works wonders;
You have manifested Your strength among the peoples.
16 By Your arm You redeemed Your people,
the children of Jacob and Joseph. *Selah*
17 The waters saw You, O God,
the waters saw You and were convulsed;
the very deep quaked as well.
18 Clouds streamed water;
the heavens rumbled;
Your arrows flew about;

[a-a] *Meaning of Heb uncertain*

19 Your thunder rumbled like wheels;
lightning lit up the world;
the earth quaked and trembled.
20 Your way was through the sea,
Your path, through the mighty waters;
Your tracks could not be seen.
21 You led Your people like a flock
in the care of Moses and Aaron.

78 A *maskil* of Asaph.

Give ear, my people, to my teaching,
turn your ear to what I say.
2 I will expound a theme,
hold forth on the lessons of the past,
3 things we have heard and known,
that our fathers have told us.
4 We will not withhold them from their children,
telling the coming generation
the praises of the LORD and His might,
and the wonders He performed.
5 He established a decree in Jacob,
ordained a teaching in Israel,
charging our fathers
to make them known to their children,
6 that a future generation might know
—children yet to be born—
and in turn tell their children
7 that they put their confidence in God,
and not forget God's great deeds,
but observe His commandments,
8 and not be like their fathers,
a wayward and defiant generation,
a generation whose heart was inconstant,
whose spirit was not true to God.

9 Like the Ephraimite bowmen
who played false in the day of battle,
10 they did not keep God's covenant,
they refused to follow His instruction;
11 they forgot His deeds
and the wonders that He showed them.
12 He performed marvels in the sight of their fathers,
in the land of Egypt, the plain of Zoan.

13 He split the sea and took them through it;
He made the waters stand like a wall.
14 He led them with a cloud by day,
and throughout the night by the light of fire.
15 He split rocks in the wilderness
and gave them drink as if from the mighty abyss.
16 He brought forth streams from a rock
and made them flow down like a river.

17 But they went on sinning against Him,
defying the Most High in the parched land.
18 To test God was in their mind
when they demanded food for themselves.
19 They spoke against God, saying,
"Can God spread a feast in the wilderness?
20 True, He struck the rock and waters flowed,
streams gushed forth;
but can He provide bread?
Can He supply His people with meat?"
21 God heard and He raged;
fire broke out against Jacob,
anger flared up at Israel,
22 because they did not put their trust in God,
did not rely on His deliverance.
23 So He commanded the skies above,
He opened the doors of heaven
24 and rained manna upon them for food,
giving them heavenly grain.
25 Each man ate a hero's meal;
He sent them provision in plenty.
26 He set the east wind moving in heaven,
and drove the south wind by His might.
27 He rained meat on them like dust,
winged birds like the sands of the sea
28 making them come down inside His camp,
around His dwelling-place.
29 They ate till they were very full;
He gave them what they craved.
30 They had not yet wearied of what they craved,
the food was still in their mouths,
31 when God's anger flared up at them.
He slew their sturdiest,
struck down the youth of Israel.

32 Nonetheless, they went on sinning

and had no faith in His wonders.
33 He made their days end in futility,
their years in sudden death.
34 When He struck[a] them, they turned to Him
and sought God once again.
35 They remembered that God was their rock,
God, most high, their redeemer.
36 Yet they deceived Him with their speech,
lied to Him with their words;
37 their hearts were inconstant toward Him;
they were untrue to His covenant.
38 But He, being merciful, forgave iniquity
and would not destroy;
He restrained His wrath time and again
and did not give full vent to His fury;
39 for He remembered that they were but flesh,
a passing breath that does not return.

40 How often did they defy Him in the wilderness,
did they grieve Him in the wasteland!
41 Again and again they tested God,
vexed[b] the Holy One of Israel.
42 They did not remember His strength,
or the day He redeemed them from the foe;
43 how He displayed His signs in Egypt,
His wonders in the plain of Zoan.
44 He turned their rivers into blood;
He made their waters undrinkable.
45 He inflicted upon them swarms of insects to devour them,
frogs to destroy them.
46 He gave their crops over to grubs,
their produce to locusts.
47 He killed their vines with hail,
their sycamores [c-]with frost.[-c]
48 He gave their beasts over to hail,
their cattle to lightning bolts.
49 He inflicted His burning anger upon them,
wrath, indignation, trouble,
a band of deadly messengers.
50 He cleared a path for His anger;
He did not stop short of slaying them,
but gave them over to pestilence.
51 He struck every firstborn in Egypt,
the first fruits of their vigor in the tents of Ham.
52 He set His people moving like sheep,

[a] *Lit. "killed"*

[b] *Or "set a limit to"*

[c-c] *Meaning of Heb uncertain*

drove them like a flock in the wilderness.
53 He led them in safety; they were unafraid;
as for their enemies, the sea covered them.
54 He brought them to His holy realm,[d]
the mountain His right hand had acquired.
55 He expelled nations before them,
[e-]settled the tribes of Israel in their tents,
allotting them their portion by the line.[-e]

56 Yet they defiantly tested God, most high,
and did not observe His decrees.
57 They fell away, disloyal like their fathers;
they played false like a treacherous bow.
58 They vexed Him with their high places;
they incensed Him with their idols.
59 God heard it and was enraged;
He utterly rejected Israel.
60 He forsook the tabernacle of Shiloh,
the tent He had set among men.
61 He let His might[f] go into captivity,
His glory into the hands of the foe.
62 He gave His people over to the sword;
He was enraged at His very own.
63 Fire consumed their young men,
and their maidens [g-]remained unwed.[-g]
64 Their priests fell by the sword
and their widows could not weep.

65 The Lord awoke as from sleep,
like a warrior [c-]shaking off[-c] wine.
66 He beat back His foes,
dealing them lasting disgrace.
67 He rejected the clan of Joseph;
He did not choose the tribe of Ephraim.
68 He did choose the tribe of Judah,
Mount Zion, which He loved.
69 He built His sanctuary like the heavens,
like the earth that He established forever.
70 He chose David, His servant,
and took him from the sheepfolds.
71 He brought him from minding the nursing ewes
to tend His people Jacob, Israel, His very own.
72 He tended them with blameless heart;
with skillful hands he led them.

[d] *Or "hill" with Greek and Saadia*

[e-e] *Inverted for clarity*

[f] *I.e. the ark; Cf. Ps. 132.8*

[g-g] *Lit. "had no nuptial song"*

[c-c] *Meaning of Heb uncertain*

79 A psalm of Asaph.

O God, heathens have entered Your domain,
defiled Your holy temple,
and turned Jerusalem into ruins.
2 They have left Your servants' corpses
as food for the fowl of heaven,
and the flesh of Your faithful for the wild beasts.
3 Their blood was shed like water around Jerusalem,
with none to bury them.
4 We have become the butt of our neighbors,
the scorn and derision of those around us.

5 How long, O LORD, will You forever be angry,
will Your indignation blaze like fire?
6 Pour Your fury on the nations that do not know You,
upon the kingdoms that do not invoke Your name,
7 for they have devoured Jacob
and desolated his home.
8 Do not hold our former iniquities against us;
let Your compassion come swiftly toward us,
for we have sunk very low.
9 Help us, O God, our deliverer,
for the sake of the glory of Your name.
Save us and forgive our sin,
for the sake of Your name.
10 Why should the nations say, "Where is their God?"
Before our eyes let it be known among the nations
that You avenge the spilled blood of Your servants.
11 Let the groans of the prisoners reach You;
reprieve those condemned to death,
as befits Your great strength.
12 Pay back our neighbors sevenfold
for the abuse they have flung at You, O LORD.
13 Then we, Your people,
the flock You shepherd,
shall glorify You forever;
for all time we shall tell Your praises.

80 For the leader; on *shoshannim, eduth.*
A psalm of Asaph.

2 Give ear, O shepherd of Israel

who leads Joseph like a flock!
Appear, You who are enthroned on the cherubim,
3 at the head of Ephraim, Benjamin, and Manasseh!
Rouse Your might and come to our help!
4 Restore us, O God;
show Your favor that we may be delivered.

5 O Lord, God of hosts,
how long will You be wrathful
toward the prayers of Your people?
6 You have fed them tears as their daily bread,
made them drink great measures of tears.
7 You set us at strife with our neighbors;
our enemies mock us at will.
8 O God of hosts, restore us;
show Your favor that we may be delivered.

9 You plucked up a vine from Egypt;
You expelled nations and planted it.
10 You cleared a place for it;
it took deep root and filled the land.
11 The mountains were covered by its shade,
mighty cedars by its boughs.
12 Its branches reached the sea,
its shoots, the river.
13 Why did You breach its wall
so that every passerby plucks its fruit,
14 wild boars gnaw at it,
and creatures of the field feed on it?

15 O God of hosts, turn again,
look down from heaven and see;
take note of that vine,
16 the stock planted by Your right hand,
the stem[a] you have taken as Your own.
17 For it is burned by fire and cut down,
perishing before Your angry blast.
18 Grant Your help[b] to the man at Your right hand,
the one You have taken as Your own.
19 We will not turn away from You;
preserve our life that we may invoke Your name.
20 O Lord, God of hosts, restore us;
show Your favor that we may be delivered.

[a] *Lit. "son"*

[b] *Lit. "hand"*

81 For the leader; on the *gittith*.
[A psalm] of Asaph.

2 Sing joyously to God, our strength;
raise a shout for the God of Jacob.
3 Take up the song,
sound the timbrel,
the melodious lyre and harp.
4 Blow the horn on the New Moon,
on the full moon for our feast day.
5 For it is a law for Israel,
a ruling of the God of Jacob;
6 He imposed it as a decree upon Joseph
when he went forth from[a] the land of Egypt;
I heard a language that I knew not.

7 I relieved his shoulder of the burden,
his hands were freed from the basket.
8 In distress you called and I rescued you;
I answered you from the [b-]secret place of thunder[-b]
I tested you at the waters of Meribah. *Selah*

9 Hear, My people, and I will admonish you;
Israel, if you would but listen to Me!
10 You shall have no foreign god,
you shall not bow to an alien god.
11 I the LORD am your God
who brought you out of the land of Egypt;
open your mouth wide and I will fill it.

12 But My people would not listen to Me,
Israel would not obey Me.
13 So I let them go after their willful heart
that they might follow their own devices.
14 If only My people would listen to Me,
if Israel would follow My paths,
15 then would I subdue their enemies at once,
strike their foes again and again.
16 Those who hate the LORD shall cower before Him;
their doom shall be eternal.
17 He fed them[c] the finest wheat;
I sated you with honey from the rock.

[a] *Or "against"*

[b-b] *Meaning of Heb uncertain*

[c] *Lit. "him," i.e. Israel*

82 A psalm of Asaph.

God stands in the divine assembly;
among the divine beings He pronounces judgment.
2 How long will you judge perversely,
showing favor to the wicked? *Selah*
3 Judge the wretched and the orphan,
vindicate the lowly and the poor,
4 rescue the wretched and the needy;
save them from the hand of the wicked.

5 They neither know nor understand,
they go about in darkness;
all the foundations of the earth totter.
6 I had taken you for divine beings,
sons of the Most High, all of you;
7 but you shall die as men do,
fall like any prince.

8 Arise, O God, judge the earth,
for all the nations are Your possession.

83 A song, a psalm of Asaph.

2 O God, do not be silent;
do not hold aloof;
do not be quiet, O God!
3 For Your enemies rage,
Your foes [a]-assert themselves.-[a]
4 They plot craftily against Your people,
take counsel against Your treasured ones.
5 They say, "Let us wipe them out as a nation;
Israel's name will be mentioned no more."
6 Unanimous in their counsel
they have made an alliance against You—
7 the clans of Edom and the Ishmaelites,
Moab and the Hagrites,
8 Gebal, Ammon, and Amalek,
Philistia with the inhabitants of Tyre;
9 Assyria too joins forces with them;
they give support to the sons of Lot. *Selah*

[a-a] *Lit. "lift up the head"*

10 Deal with them as You did with Midian,
with Sisera, with Jabin,
at the Brook Kishon—
11 who were destroyed at En-dor,
who became dung for the field.
12 Treat their great men like Oreb and Zeeb,
all their princes like Zebah and Zalmunna,
13 who said, "Let us take the meadows of God as our possession."
14 O my God, make them like thistledown,
like stubble driven by the wind.
15 As a fire burns a forest,
as flames scorch the hills,
16 pursue them with Your tempest,
terrify them with Your storm.
17 Cover[b] their faces with shame
so that they seek Your name, O LORD.
18 May they be frustrated and terrified,
disgraced and doomed forever.
19 May they know
that Your name, Yours alone, is the LORD,
supreme over all the earth.

[b] *Lit. "fill"*

84

For the leader; on the *gittith*.
A psalm of the Korahites.

2 How lovely is Your dwelling-place,
O LORD of hosts.
3 I long, I yearn for the courts of the LORD;
my body and soul shout for joy to the living God.
4 Even the sparrow has found a home,
and the swallow a nest for herself
in which to set her young,
near Your altar, O LORD of hosts,
my king and my God.
5 Happy are those who dwell in Your house;
they forever praise You. *Selah*

6 Happy is the man who finds refuge in You,
whose mind is on the [pilgrim] highways.
7 They pass through the Valley of Baca,
[a]regarding it as a place of springs,
as if the early rain had covered it with blessing.[a]
8 They go from [b]rampart to rampart,[b]
appearing before God in Zion.

[a-a] *Meaning of Heb uncertain*
[b-b] *Others "strength to strength"*

9 O LORD, God of hosts,
hear my prayer;
give ear, O God of Jacob. *Selah*
10 O God, behold our shield,
look upon the face of Your anointed.

11 Better one day in Your courts than a thousand [anywhere else];
I would rather stand at the threshold of God's house
than dwell in the tents of the wicked.
12 For the LORD God is sun[c] and shield;
the LORD bestows grace and glory;
He does not withhold His bounty from those who live without blame.

[c] *Or "bulwark," with Targ.*

13 O LORD of hosts,
happy is the man who trusts in You.

85

For the leader.
A psalm of the Korahites.

2 O LORD, You [a-]will favor[-a] Your land,
restore[b] Jacob's fortune;
3 You [c-]will forgive[-c] Your people's iniquity,
pardon[d] all their sins; *Selah*
4 You [e-]will withdraw[-e] all Your anger,
turn[f] away from Your rage.
5 Turn again, O God, our helper,
revoke Your displeasure with us.
6 Will You be angry with us forever,
prolong Your wrath for all generations?
7 Surely You will revive us again,
so that Your people may rejoice in You.
8 Show us, O LORD, Your faithfulness;
grant us Your deliverance.

[a-a] *Or "have favored"*
[b] *Or "have restored"*
[c-c] *Or "have forgiven"*
[d] *Or "have pardoned"*
[e-e] *Or "have withdrawn"*
[f] *Or "have turned"*

9 Let me hear what God, the LORD, will speak;
He will promise well-being to His people, His faithful ones;
may they not turn to folly.
10 His help is very near to those who fear Him,
to make His glory dwell in our land.
11 Faithfulness and truth meet;
justice and well-being kiss.
12 Truth springs up from the earth;
justice looks down from heaven.
13 The LORD also bestows His bounty;

our land yields its produce.
14 Justice goes before Him
as He sets out on His way.

86 A prayer of David.

Incline Your ear, O LORD,
answer me
for I am poor and needy.
2 Preserve my life for I am steadfast;
O You, my God,
deliver Your servant who trusts in You.
3 Have mercy on me, O my LORD,
for I call to You all day long;
4 bring joy to Your servant's life,
for on You, my LORD, I set my hope.
5 For You, my LORD, are good and forgiving,
abounding in steadfast love to all who call on You.
6 Give ear, O LORD, to my prayer;
heed my plea for mercy.
7 In my time of trouble I call You,
for You will answer me.

8 There is none like You among the gods, O my LORD,
and there are no deeds like Yours.
9 All the nations You have made
will come to bow down before You, O my LORD,
and they will pay honor to Your name.
10 For You are great and perform wonders;
You alone are God.

11 Teach me Your way, O LORD;
I will walk in Your truth;
let my heart be undivided in the worship of You.[a]
12 I will praise You, O LORD, my God, with all my heart
and pay honor to Your name forever.
13 For Your steadfast love toward me is great;
You save me from the depths of Sheol.

14 O God, arrogant men have risen against me;
a band of ruthless men seek my life;
they are not mindful of You.
15 But You, O my LORD, are a God
compassionate and merciful,

[a] *Lit. "Your name"*

slow to anger, abounding in steadfast love and faithfulness.
16 Turn to me and have mercy on me;
grant Your strength to Your servant
and deliver the son of Your maidservant.
17 Show me a sign of Your favor,
that my enemies may see and be frustrated
because You, O LORD, have given me aid and comfort.

87[a]

1-2 A psalm of the Korahites, a song.

[a] The meaning of many passages in this psalm is uncertain

The LORD loves the gates of Zion,
His foundation on the holy mountains,
more than all the dwellings of Jacob.
3 Glorious things are spoken of you,
O city of God. *Selah*
4 I mention Rahab[b] and Babylon among those who acknowledge Me;
Philistia, and Tyre, and Cush—each was born there.
5 Indeed, it shall be said of Zion,
"Every man was born there."
[c]-He, the Most High, will preserve it.-[c]
6 The LORD will inscribe in the register of peoples
that each was born there. *Selah*
7 Singers and dancers alike [will say]:
"All my roots[d] are in You."

[b] *a poetic term for Egypt; cf. Isa. 30.7*

[c-c] *Or "He will preserve it supreme"*

[d] *Lit. "sources"*

88

A song, a psalm of the Korahites.
For the leader; [a]-on *mahalath leannoth.*-[a]
A *maskil* of Heman the Ezrahite.

[a-a] *Meaning of Heb uncertain*

2 O LORD, God of my deliverance,
[b]-when I cry out in the night-[b] before You,
3 let my prayer reach You;
incline Your ear to my cry.
4 For I am sated with misfortune;
I am at the brink of Sheol.
5 I am numbered with those who go down to the Pit;
I am a helpless man
6 abandoned[c] among the dead,
like bodies lying in the grave
of whom You are mindful no more,
and who are cut off from Your care.
7 You have put me at the bottom of the Pit,
in the darkest places, in the depths.

[b-b] *Or "by day I cry out [and] by night"*

[c] *Lit. "released"*

8 Your fury lies heavy upon me;
You afflict me with all Your breakers. *Selah*
9 You make my companions shun me;
You make me abhorrent to them;
I am shut in and do not go out.
10 My eyes pine away from affliction;
I call to You, O LORD, each day;
I stretch out my hands to You.

11 Do You work wonders for the dead?
Do the shades rise to praise You? *Selah*
12 Is Your faithful care recounted in the grave,
Your constancy in the place of perdition?
13 Are Your wonders made known in the Underworld,[d]
Your beneficent deeds in the land of oblivion?

14 As for me, I cry out to You;
each morning my prayer greets You.
15 Why, O LORD, do You reject me,
do You hide Your face from me?
16 From my youth I have been afflicted
and near death;
I suffer Your terrors [e]wherever I turn.[e]
17 Your fury overwhelms me;
Your terrors destroy me.
18 They swirl about me like waters all day long;
they encircle me on every side.
19 You have put friend and neighbor far from me
and my companions out of my sight.[f]

[d] *Lit. "darkness"*

[e-e] *Following Saadia; meaning of Heb uncertain*

[f] *Lit. "into darkness"*

89

A *maskil* of Ethan the Ezrahite.

2 I will sing of the LORD's steadfast love forever;
to all generations I will proclaim Your faithfulness with my mouth.
3 I declare, "Your steadfast love is confirmed forever;
there in the heavens You establish Your faithfulness."

4 "I have made a covenant with My chosen one;
I have sworn to My servant David:
5 I will establish your offspring forever,
I will confirm your throne for all generations." *Selah*

6 Your wonders, O LORD, are praised by the heavens,
Your faithfulness, too, in the assembly of holy beings.

7 For who in the skies can equal the LORD,
can compare with the LORD among the divine beings,
8 a God greatly dreaded in the council of holy beings,
awesome to all around Him?
9 O LORD, God of hosts,
who is mighty like You, O LORD?
Your faithfulness surrounds You;
10 You rule the swelling of the sea;
when its waves surge, You still them.
11 You crushed Rahab; he was like a corpse;
with Your powerful arm You scattered Your enemies.
12 The heaven is Yours,
the earth too;
the world and all it holds—
You established them.
13 North and south—
You created them;
Tabor and Hermon sing forth Your name.
14 Yours is an arm endowed with might;
Your hand is strong;
Your right hand, exalted.
15 Righteousness and justice are the base of Your throne;
steadfast love and faithfulness stand before You.

16 Happy is the people who know the joyful shout;
O LORD, they walk in the light of Your presence.
17 They rejoice in Your name all day long;
they are exalted through Your righteousness.
18 For You are their strength in which they glory;
our horn is exalted through Your favor.
19 Truly the LORD is our shield,
the Holy One of Israel our king.

20 Then[a] You spoke to Your faithful ones in a vision
and said, "I have conferred power upon a warrior;
I have exalted one chosen out of the people.
21 I have found David, My servant;
anointed him with My sacred oil.
22 My hand shall be constantly with him,
and My arm shall strengthen him.
23 No enemy shall [b-]oppress him,[-b]
no vile man afflict him.
24 I will crush his adversaries before him;
I will strike down those who hate him.
25 My faithfulness and steadfast love shall be with him;

[a] *Referring to vv. 4–5; cf. II Sam. 7.1–17*

[b-b] *Meaning of Heb uncertain*

his horn shall be exalted through My name.
26 I will set his hand upon the sea,
his right hand upon the rivers.
27 He shall say to Me,
'You are my father, my God, the rock of my deliverance.'
28 I will appoint him firstborn,
highest of the kings of the earth.
29 I will maintain My steadfast love for him always;
My covenant with him shall endure.
30 I will establish his line forever,
his throne, as long as the heavens last.
31 If his sons forsake My teaching
and do not live by My rules;
32 if they violate My laws,
and do not observe My commands,
33 I will punish their transgression with the rod,
their iniquity with plagues.
34 But I will not take away My steadfast love from him;
I will not betray My faithfulness.
35 I will not violate My covenant,
or change what I have uttered.
36 I have sworn by My holiness, once and for all;
I will not be false to David.
37 His line shall continue forever,
his throne, as the sun before Me,
38 as the moon, established forever,
an enduring witness in the sky." *Selah*

39 Yet You have rejected, spurned,
and become enraged at Your anointed.
40 You have repudiated the covenant with Your servant;
You have dragged his dignity in the dust.
41 You have breached all his defenses,
shattered his strongholds.
42 All who pass by plunder him;
he has become the butt of his neighbors.
43 You have exalted the right hand of his adversaries,
and made all his enemies rejoice.
44 You have turned back the blade of his sword,
and have not sustained him in battle.
45 You have brought [b-]his splendor[-b] to an end
and have hurled his throne to the ground.
46 You have cut short the days of his youth;
You have covered him with shame. *Selah*

[b-b] *Meaning of Heb uncertain*

47 How long, O LORD, will You forever hide Your face,
will Your fury blaze like fire?
48 O remember [b-]how short my life is;[-b]
why should You have created every man in vain?
49 What man can live and not see death,
can save himself from the clutches of Sheol? *Selah*
50 O LORD, where is Your steadfast love of old
which You swore to David in Your faithfulness?
51 Remember, O LORD, the abuse flung at Your servants
[b-]that I have borne in my bosom [from] many peoples,[-b]
52 how Your enemies, O LORD, have flung abuse,
abuse at Your anointed at every step.

[b-b] *Meaning of Heb uncertain*

53 Blessed is the LORD forever;
Amen and Amen.

BOOK FOUR

90

A prayer of Moses, the man of God.

O Lord, You have been our refuge in every generation.
2 Before the mountains came into being,
before You brought forth the earth and the world,
from eternity to eternity You are God.

3 You return man to dust;[a]
You decreed, "Return you mortals!"
4 [b-]For in Your sight a thousand years
are like yesterday that has past,
like a watch of the night.
5 You engulf men in sleep;[-b]
at daybreak they are like grass that renews itself;
6 at daybreak it flourishes anew;
at dusk it withers and dries up.
7 So we are consumed by Your anger,
terror-struck by Your fury.
8 You have set our iniquities before You,
our hidden sins in the light of Your face.
9 All our days pass away in Your wrath;
we spend our years like a sigh.
10 The span of our life is seventy years,
or, given the strength, eighty years;

[a] *Or "contrition"*

[b-b] *Meaning of Heb uncertain*

but the [b]best of them[b] are trouble and sorrow.
They pass by speedily, and we [c]are in darkness.[c]
11 Who can know Your furious anger?
Your wrath matches the fear of You.
12 Teach us to count our days rightly,
that we may obtain a wise heart.

13 Turn, O LORD!
How long?
Show mercy to Your servants.
14 Satisfy us at daybreak with Your steadfast love
that we may sing for joy all our days.
15 Give us joy for as long as You have afflicted us,
for the years we have suffered misfortune.
16 Let Your deeds be seen by Your servants,
Your glory by their children.
17 May the favor of the LORD be upon us;
let all that we put our hands to prosper,
O prosper the work of our hands!

b-b *Meaning of Heb uncertain*
c-c *Or "fly away"*

91

O you who dwell in the shelter of the Most High
and abide in the protection of Shaddai—
2 I say of the LORD, my refuge and stronghold,
my God in whom I trust,
3 that He will save you from the fowler's trap,
from the destructive plague.
4 He will cover you with His pinions;
you will find refuge under His wings;
His fidelity is an encircling shield.
5 You need not fear the terror by night,
or the arrow that flies by day,
6 the plague that stalks in the darkness,
or the scourge that ravages at noon.
7 A thousand may fall at your left side,
ten thousand at your right,
but it shall not reach you.
8 You will see it with your eyes,
you will witness the punishment of the wicked.
9 Beause you took the LORD, my refuge,
the Most High, as your haven,
10 no harm will befall you,
no disease touch your tent.
11 For He will order His angels
to guard you wherever you go.

12 They will carry you in their hands
lest you hurt your foot on a stone.
13 You will tread on cubs and vipers;
you will trample lions and asps.

14 "Because he is devoted to Me I will deliver him;
I will keep him safe, for he knows My name.
15 When he calls on Me, I will answer him;
I will be with him in distress;
I will rescue him and honor him;
16 I will let him live to a ripe old age,
and show him My salvation."

92 A psalm, a song; for the sabbath day.

2 It is good to praise the LORD,
to sing hymns to Your name, O Most High,
3 To proclaim Your steadfast love at daybreak,
Your faithfulness each night
4 With the ten-stringed harp,
with voice and lyre together.

5 You have gladdened me by Your deeds, O LORD;
I shout for joy at Your handiwork.
6 How great are Your works, O LORD,
how very subtle[a] Your designs!
7 A brutish man cannot know,
a fool cannot understand this:
8 though the wicked bloom, they are like grass;
though all evildoers blossom,
it is only that they may be destroyed forever.

9 But You are exalted, O LORD, for all time.

10 Lo, Your enemies, O LORD,
lo, Your enemies perish;
all evildoers are scattered.
11 You raise my horn high like that of a wild ox;
I am soaked in freshening oil.
12 I shall see the defeat of my watchful foes,
hear of the downfall of the wicked who beset me.
13 The righteous bloom like a date-palm;
they thrive like a cedar in Lebanon;
14 planted in the house of the LORD,

[a] *Meaning of Heb uncertain*

they flourish in the courts of our God.
15 In old age they still produce fruit;
they are full of sap and freshness,
16 attesting that the LORD is upright,
my rock, in whom there is no wrong.

93

The LORD is king,
He is robed in grandeur;
the LORD is robed,
He is girded with strength.
The world stands firm;
it cannot be shaken.
2 Your throne stands firm from of old;
from eternity You have existed.
3 The ocean sounds, O LORD,
the ocean sounds its thunder,
the ocean sounds its pounding.
4 Above the thunder of the mighty waters,
more majestic than the breakers of the sea
is the LORD, majestic on high.
5 Your decrees are indeed enduring;
holiness befits Your house,
O LORD, for all times.

94

God of vengeance, LORD,
God of vengeance, appear!
2 Rise up, judge of the earth,
give the arrogant their deserts!
3 How long shall the wicked, O LORD,
how long shall the wicked exult,
4 shall they utter insolent speech,
shall all evildoers vaunt themselves?
5 They crush Your people, O LORD,
they afflict Your very own;
6 they kill the widow and the stranger;
they murder the fatherless,
7 thinking, "The LORD does not see it,
the God of Jacob does not pay heed."

8 Take heed, you most brutish people;
fools, when will you get wisdom?
9 Shall He who implants the ear not hear,
He who forms the eye not see?

10 Shall He who disciplines nations not punish,
He who instructs men in knowledge?
11 The LORD knows the designs of men to be futile.

12 Happy is the man whom You discipline, O LORD,
the man You instruct in Your teaching,
13 to give him tranquillity in times of misfortune,
until a pit be dug for the wicked.
14 For the LORD will not forsake His people;
He will not abandon His very own.
15 Judgment shall again accord with justice
and all the upright shall rally to it.

16 Who will take my part against evil men?
Who will stand up for me against wrongdoers?
17 Were not the LORD my help,
I should soon dwell in silence.
18 When I think my foot has given way,
Your faithfulness, O LORD, supports me.
19 When I am filled with cares,
Your assurance soothes my soul.

20 Shall the seat of injustice be Your partner,
that frames mischief by statute?
21 They band together to do away with the righteous;
they condemn the innocent to death.
22 But the LORD is my haven;
my God is my sheltering rock.
23 He will make their evil recoil upon them,
annihilate them through their own wickedness;
the LORD our God will annihilate them.

95

Come, let us sing joyously to the LORD,
raise a shout for our rock and deliverer;
2 let us come into His presence with praise;
let us raise a shout for Him in song!
3 For the LORD is a great God,
the great king of all divine beings.
4 In His hand are the depths of the earth;
the peaks of the mountains are His.
5 His is the sea, He made it;
and the land, which His hands fashioned.

6 Come, let us bow down and kneel,

bend the knee before the LORD our maker,
7 for He is our God,
and we are the people He tends, the flock in His hand.
O, if you would but heed His charge this day:
8 do not be stubborn as at Meribah,
as on the day of Massah, in the wilderness,
9 when your fathers put Me to the test,
tried Me, though they had seen My deeds.
10 Forty years I was provoked by that generation;
I thought, "They are a senseless people;
they would not know My ways."
11 Concerning them I swore in anger,
"They shall never come to My resting-place!"

96[a]

Sing to the LORD a new song,
sing to the LORD, all the earth.
2 Sing to the LORD, bless His name,
proclaim His victory day after day.
3 Tell of His glory among the nations,
His wondrous deeds, among all peoples.
4 For the LORD is great and much acclaimed,
He is held in awe by all divine beings.
5 All the gods of the nations are mere idols,
but the LORD made the heavens.
6 Glory and majesty are before Him;
strength and splendor are in His temple.

7 Ascribe to the LORD, O families of the peoples,
ascribe to the LORD glory and strength.
8 Ascribe to the LORD the glory of His name,
bring tribute and enter His courts.
9 Bow down to the LORD majestic in holiness;
tremble in His presence, all the earth!
10 Declare among the nations, "The LORD is king!"
the world stands firm; it cannot be shaken;
He judges the peoples with equity.
11 Let the heavens rejoice and the earth exult;
let the sea and all within it thunder,
12 the fields and everything in them exult;
then shall all the trees of the forest shout for joy
13 at the presence of the LORD, for He is coming,
for He is coming to rule the earth;
He will rule the world justly
and its peoples in faithfulness.

[a] *Cf. I Chron. 16.23–33*

97 The LORD is king!
Let the earth exult,
the many islands rejoice!
2 Dense clouds are around Him,
righteousness and justice are the base of His throne.
3 Fire is His vanguard,
burning His foes on every side.
4 His lightnings light up the world;
the earth is convulsed at the sight;
5 mountains melt like wax at the LORD's presence,
at the presence of the Lord of all the earth.
6 The heavens proclaim His righteousness
and all peoples see His glory.
7 All who worship images,
who vaunt their idols,
are dismayed;
all divine beings bow down to Him.
8 Zion, hearing it, rejoices,
the towns[a] of Judah exult,
because of Your judgments, O LORD.
9 For You, LORD, are supreme over all the earth;
You are exalted high above all divine beings.

10 O you who love the LORD, hate evil!
He guards the lives of His loyal ones,
saving them from the hand of the wicked.
11 Light is sown for the righteous,
radiance[b] for the upright.
12 O you righteous, rejoice in the LORD
and acclaim His holy name!

[a] *Or "women"*

[b] *Others "joy"*

98 A psalm.

Sing to the LORD a new song
for He has worked wonders;
His right hand, His holy arm,
has won Him victory.
2 The LORD has manifested His victory,
has displayed His triumph in the sight of the nations.
3 He was mindful of His steadfast love and faithfulness
toward the house of Israel;
all the ends of the earth beheld the victory of our God.

4 Raise a shout to the LORD, all the earth,
break into joyous songs of praise!
5 Sing praise to the LORD with the lyre,
with the lyre and melodious song.
6 With trumpets and the blast of the horn
raise a shout before the LORD, the king.
7 Let the sea and all within it thunder,
the world and its inhabitants;
8 let the rivers clap their hands,
the mountains sing joyously together
9 at the presence of the LORD,
for He is coming to rule the earth;
He will rule the world justly,
and its peoples with equity.

99

[a-]The LORD, enthroned on cherubim, is king,
peoples tremble, the earth quakes.[-a]
2 The LORD is great in Zion,
and exalted above all peoples.
3 They praise Your name as great and awesome;
He is holy!

4 [b-]Mighty king[-b] who loves justice,
it was You who established equity,
You who worked righteous judgment in Jacob.
5 Exalt the LORD our God
and bow down to His footstool;
He is holy!

6 Moses and Aaron were among His priests,
Samuel, among those who call on His name;
when they called to the LORD,
He answered them.
7 He spoke to them in a pillar of cloud;
they obeyed His decrees,
the law He gave them.
8 O LORD our God, You answered them;
You were a sustaining[c] God for them,
avenging their injuries.

9 Exalt the LORD our God,
and bow toward His holy hill,
for the LORD our God is holy.

[a-a] *Clauses transposed for clarity*

[b-b] *Meaning of Heb uncertain*

[c] *Or "forgiving"*

100 A psalm [a]for praise.[a]

[a-a] *Traditionally, "for the thanksgiving offering"*

Raise a shout for the LORD, all the earth;
2 worship the LORD in gladness;
come into His presence with shouts of joy.
3 Acknowledge that the LORD is God;
He made us and [b]we are His,[b]
His people, the flock He tends.
4 Enter His gates with praise,
His courts with acclamation.
Praise Him!
Bless His name!
5 For the LORD is good;
His steadfast love is eternal;
His faithfulness is for all generations.

[b-b] *So* Qere; Ketib *and some ancient versions: "not we ourselves"*

101 A psalm of David.

I will sing of faithfulness and justice;
I will chant a hymn to You, O LORD.
2 I will study the way of the blameless;
when shall I attain it?
I will live without blame within my house.
3 I will not set before my eyes anything base;
I hate crooked dealing;
I will have none of it.
4 Perverse thoughts will be far from me;
I will know nothing of evil.
5 He who slanders his friend in secret will I destroy;
I cannot endure the haughty and presumptuous.
6 My eyes are on the trusty men of the land,
to have them at my side.
He who follows the way of the blameless,
will be in my service.
7 He who deals deceitfully
shall not live in my house;
he who speaks untruth
shall not stand before my eyes.
8 Each morning I will destroy
all the wicked of the land,
To rid the city of the LORD
of all evildoers.

102 A prayer of the lowly man when he is faint and pours forth his plea before the LORD.

2 O LORD, hear my prayer;
let my cry come before You.
3 Do not hide Your face from me
in my time of trouble;
turn Your ear to me;
when I cry, answer me speedily.
4 For my days have vanished like smoke
and my body is charred like a hearth.
5 I am stricken and withered like grass;
[a]too wasted[a] to eat my food;
6 on account of my vehement groaning
my bones [b]show through my skin.[b]
7 I am like a great-owl in the wilderness,
an owl among the ruins.
8 I lie awake; I am like
a lone bird upon a roof.
9 All day long my enemies revile me;
my deriders use my name to curse.
10 For I have eaten ashes like bread
and mixed my drink with tears,
11 because of Your wrath and Your fury;
for You have cast me far away.
12 My days are like a lengthening shadow;
I wither like grass.

13 But You, O LORD, are enthroned forever;
Your fame endures throughout the ages.
14 You will surely arise and take pity on Zion,
for it is time to be gracious to her;
the appointed time has come.
15 Your servants take delight in its stones,
and cherish its dust.
16 The nations will fear the name of the LORD,
all the kings of the earth, Your glory.
17 For the LORD has built Zion;
He has appeared in all His glory.
18 He has turned to the prayer [c]of the destitute[c]
and has not spurned their prayer.
19 May this be written down for a coming generation,
that people yet to be created may praise the LORD.
20 For He looks down from His holy height;

[a-a] *Others "forget"*

[b-b] *Lit. "cling to my flesh"*

[c-c] *Meaning of Heb uncertain*

the LORD beholds the earth from heaven
21 to hear the groans of the prisoner,
to release those condemned to death;
22 that the fame of the LORD may be recounted in Zion,
His praises in Jerusalem,
23 when the nations gather together,
the kingdoms, to serve the LORD.

24 He drained my strength in mid-course,
He shortened my days.
25 I say, "O my God, do not take me away
in the middle of my life,
You whose years endure generations on end.
26 Of old You established the earth;
the heavens are the work of Your hands.
27 They shall perish, but You shall endure;
they shall all wear out like a garment;
You change them like clothing and they pass away.
28 But You are He whose years are without end.
29 May the children of Your servants dwell securely
and their offspring endure in Your presence."

103 [A psalm] of David.

Bless the LORD, O my soul,
all my being, His holy name.
2 Bless the LORD, O my soul
and do not forget all His bounties.
3 He forgives all your sins,
heals all your diseases.
4 He redeems your life from the Pit,
surrounds you with steadfast love and mercy.
5 He satisfies you with good things in [a-]the prime of life,[-a]
so that your youth is renewed like the eagle's.

[a-a] *Meaning of Heb uncertain*

6 The LORD executes righteous acts
and judgments for all who are wronged.
7 He made known His ways to Moses,
His deeds to the children of Israel.
8 The LORD is compassionate and gracious,
slow to anger, abounding in steadfast love.
9 He will not contend forever,
or nurse His anger for all time.
10 He has not dealt with us according to our sins,

nor has He requited us according to our iniquities.
11 For as the heavens are high above the earth,
so great is His steadfast love toward those who fear Him.
12 As east is far from west,
so far has He removed our sins from us.
13 As a father has compassion for his children,
so the Lord has compassion for those who fear Him.
14 For He knows how we are formed;
He is mindful that we are dust.

15 Man's days are like grass;
he blooms like a flower of the field;
16 a wind passes by and it is no more,
its own place no longer knows it.
17 But the LORD's steadfast love is for all eternity
toward those who fear Him,
and His beneficence is for the children's children
18 of those who keep His covenant
and remember to observe His precepts.
19 The LORD has established His throne in heaven,
and His sovereign rule is over all.

20 Bless the LORD, O His angels,
mighty creatures who do His bidding,
ever obedient to His bidding;
21 bless the LORD, all His hosts,
His servants who do His will;
22 bless the LORD, all His works,
through the length and breadth of His realm;
bless the LORD, O my soul.

104

Bless the LORD, O my soul;
O LORD, my God, You are very great;
You are clothed in glory and majesty,
2 wrapped in a robe of light;
You spread the heavens like a tent cloth.
3 He sets the rafters of His lofts in the waters,
makes the clouds His chariot,
moves on the wings of the wind.
4 He makes the winds His messengers,
fiery flames His servants.
5 He established the earth on its foundations,
so that it shall never totter.
6 You made the deep cover it as a garment;

the waters stood above the mountains.
7 They fled at Your blast,
rushed away at the sound of Your thunder,
8 up the mountains, down the valleys,
to the place You established for them.
9 You set bounds they must not pass
so that they never again cover the earth.

10 You make springs gush forth in torrents;
they make their way between the hills,
11 giving drink to all the wild beasts;
the wild asses slake their thirst.
12 The birds of the sky dwell beside them
and sing among the foliage.
13 You water the mountains from Your[a] lofts;
the earth is sated from the fruit of Your work.
14 You make the grass grow for the cattle
and herbage for man's labor,
that he may get food out of the earth—
15 wine that cheers the hearts of men
[b-]oil that makes the face shine,[-b]
and bread that sustains man's life.
16 The trees of the LORD drink their fill,
the cedars of Lebanon, His own planting,
17 where birds make their nests;
the stork has her home in the junipers.
18 The high mountains are for wild goats;
the crags are a refuge for rock-badgers.

19 He made the moon to mark the seasons;
the sun knows when to set.
20 You bring on darkness and it is night,
when all the beasts of the forests stir.
21 The lions roar for prey,
seeking their food from God.
22 When the sun rises, they come home
and couch in their dens.
23 Man then goes out to his work,
to his labor until the evening.

24 How many are the things You have made, O LORD;
You have made them all with wisdom;
the earth is full of Your creations.
25 There is the sea, vast and wide,
with its creatures beyond number,

[a] *Lit. "His"*

[b-b] *Lit. "to make the face shine from oil"*

livings things, small and great.
26 There go the ships,
and Leviathan that You formed to sport with.
27 All of them look to You
to give them their food when it is due.
28 Give it to them, they gather it up;
open Your hand, they are well satisfied;
29 hide Your face, they are terrified;
take away their breath, they perish
and turn again into dust;
30 send back Your breath, they are created,
and You renew the face of the earth.

31 May the glory of the LORD endure forever;
may the LORD rejoice in His works!
32 He looks at the earth and it trembles;
He touches the mountains and they smoke.

33 I will sing to the LORD as long as I live;
all my life I will chant hymns to my God.
34 May my prayer be pleasing to Him;
I will rejoice in the LORD.
35 May sinners disappear from the earth,
and the wicked be no more.
Bless the LORD, O my soul.
Hallelujah.

105

Praise the LORD;
call on His name;
proclaim His deeds among the nations.
2 Sing praises unto Him;
speak of all His wondrous acts.
3 Exult in His holy name;
let all who seek the LORD rejoice.
4 Turn to the LORD, to His might;[a]
seek His presence constantly.
5 Remember the wonders He has done;
His portents and the judgments He has pronounced,
6 O offspring of Abraham, His servant,
O descendants of Jacob, His chosen ones.

7 He is the LORD our God;
His judgments are throughout the earth.
8 He is ever mindful of His covenant,

[a] *I.e. the ark; cf. Ps 78. 61; 132. 8*

the promise He gave for a thousand generations,
9 that He made with Abraham,
swore to Isaac,
10 and confirmed in a decree for Jacob,
for Israel, as an eternal covenant,
11 saying, "To you I will give the land of Canaan
as your allotted heritage."

12 They were then few in number,
a handful, merely sojourning there,
13 wandering from nation to nation,
from one kingdom to another.
14 He allowed no one to oppress them;
He reproved kings on their account,
15 "Do not touch My anointed ones;
do not harm My prophets."

16 He called down a famine on the land,
destroyed every staff of bread.
17 He sent ahead of them a man,
Joseph, sold into slavery.
18 His feet were subjected to fetters;
an iron collar was put on his neck.
19 Until his prediction came true
the decree of the LORD purged him.
20 The king sent to have him freed;
the ruler of nations released him.
21 He made him the lord of his household,
empowered him over all his possessions,
22 to discipline his princes at will,
to teach his elders wisdom.
23 Then Israel came to Egypt;
Jacob dwelt in the land of Ham.

24 He made His people very fruitful,
more numerous than their foes.
25 He changed their heart[b] to hate His people,
to plot against His servants.
26 He sent His servant Moses,
and Aaron, whom He had chosen.
27 They performed His signs among them,
His wonders, against the land of Ham.
28 He sent darkness; it was very dark;
[c-]did they not defy His word?[-c]
29 He turned their waters into blood

[b] *Or "Their heart changed"*

[c-c] *Meaning of Heb uncertain*

and killed their fish.
30 Their land teemed with frogs,
even the rooms of their king.
31 Swarms of insects came at His command,
lice throughout their country.
32 He gave them hail for rain,
and flaming fire in their land.
33 He struck their vines and fig trees,
broke down the trees of their country.
34 Locusts came at His command,
grasshoppers without number.
35 They devoured every green thing in the land;
they consumed the produce of the soil.
36 He struck down every firstborn in the land,
the first fruit of their vigor.
37 He led Israel[d] out with silver and gold;
none among their tribes faltered.
38 Egypt rejoiced when they left,
for dread of Israel[d] had fallen upon them.

[d] *Lit. "them"*

39 He spread a cloud for a cover,
and fire to light up the night.
40 They asked and He brought them quail,
and satisfied them with food from heaven.
41 He opened a rock so that water gushed forth;
it flowed as a stream in the parched land.
42 Mindful of His sacred promise
to His servant Abraham,
43 He led His people out in gladness,
His chosen ones with joyous song.
44 He gave them the lands of nations;
they inherited the wealth of peoples,
45 that they might keep His laws
and observe His teachings.
Hallelujah.

106

Hallelujah.
Praise the LORD for He is good;
His steadfast love is eternal.
2 Who can tell the mighty acts of the LORD,
proclaim all His praises?

3 Happy are those who act justly,
who do right at all times.

4 Be mindful of me, O LORD, when You favor Your people;
take note of me when You deliver them,
5 that I may enjoy the prosperity of Your chosen ones,
share in the joy of Your nation,
glory in Your very own people.

6 We have sinned like our forefathers;
we have gone astray, done evil.
7 Our forefathers in Egypt did not perceive Your wonders;
they did not remember Your abundant love,
but rebelled at the sea, at the Sea of Reeds.
8 Yet He saved them, as befits His name,
to make known His might.
9 He sent His blast against the Sea of Reeds;
it became dry;
He led them through the deep as through a wilderness.
10 He delivered them from the foe,
redeemed them from the enemy.
11 Water covered their adversaries;
not one of them was left.
12 Then they believed His promise,
and sang His praises.
13 But they soon forgot His deeds;
they would not wait to learn His plan.
14 They were seized with craving in the wilderness,
and put God to the test in the wasteland.
15 He gave them what they asked for,
then made them waste away.
16 There was envy of Moses in the camp,
and of Aaron, the holy one of the LORD.
17 The earth opened up and swallowed Dathan,
closed over the party of Abiram.
18 A fire blazed among their party,
a flame that consumed the wicked.
19 They made a calf at Horeb
and bowed down to a molten image.
20 They exchanged their glory
for the image of a bull that feeds on grass.
21 They forgot God who saved them,
who performed great deeds in Egypt,
22 wondrous deeds in the land of Ham,
awesome deeds at the Sea of Reeds.
23 He would have destroyed them
had not Moses His chosen one
confronted Him in the breach

to avert His destructive wrath.
24 They rejected the desirable land,
and put no faith in His promise.
25 They grumbled in their tents
and disobeyed the LORD.
26 So He raised His hand in oath
to make them fall in the wilderness,
27 to disperse[a] their offspring among the nations
and scatter them through the lands.
28 They attached themselves to Baal Peor,
ate sacrifices offered to the dead.
29 They provoked anger by their deeds,
and a plague broke out among them.
30 Phineas stepped forth and intervened,
and the plague ceased.
31 It was reckoned to his merit
for all generations, to eternity.
32 They provoked wrath at the waters of Meribah
and Moses suffered on their account,
33 because they rebelled against Him
and he spoke rashly.

34 They did not destroy the nations
as the LORD had commanded them,
35 but mingled with the nations
and learned their ways.
36 They worshiped their idols,
which became a snare for them.
37 Their own sons and daughters
they sacrificed to demons.
38 They shed innocent blood,
the blood of their sons and daughters,
whom they sacrificed to the idols of Canaan;
so the land was polluted with bloodguilt.
39 Thus they became defiled by their acts,
debauched through their deeds.
40 The LORD was angry with His people
and He abhorred His inheritance.
41 He handed them over to the nations;
their foes ruled them.
42 Their enemies oppressed them
and they were subject to their power.
43 He saved them time and again,
but they were deliberately rebellious,
and so they were brought low by their iniquity.

[a] *Cf. Targ., Kimhi*

44 When He saw that they were in distress,
when He heard their cry,
45 He was mindful of His covenant
and in His great faithfulness relented.
46 He made all their captors kindly disposed toward them.

47 Save us, O LORD our God,
and gather us from among the nations,
to acclaim Your holy name,
to glory in Your praise.

48 Blessed is the LORD, God of Israel, to all eternity.
Let all the people say, "Amen."
Hallelujah.

BOOK FIVE

107

"Praise the LORD for He is good;
His steadfast love is eternal!"
2 So let those redeemed by the LORD say,
those He redeemed from adversity,
3 whom He gathered in from the lands,
from east and west,
from the north and from the sea.

4 Some lost their way in the wilderness,
in the wasteland;
they found no settled place.
5 Hungry and thirsty,
their spirit failed.
6 In their adversity they cried to the LORD,
and He rescued them from their troubles.
7 He showed them a direct way
to reach a settled place.
8 Let them praise the LORD for His steadfast love,
His wondrous deeds for mankind;
9 for He has satisfied the thirsty,
filled the hungry with all good things.

10 Some lived in deepest darkness,
bound in cruel irons,
11 because they defied the word of God,

spurned the counsel of the Most High.
12 He humbled their hearts through suffering;
they stumbled with no one to help.
13 In their adversity they cried to the LORD,
and He rescued them from their troubles.
14 He brought them out of deepest darkness,
broke their bonds asunder.
15 Let them praise the LORD for His steadfast love,
His wondrous deeds for mankind,
16 For He shattered gates of brass,
He broke their iron bars.

17 There were fools who suffered for their sinful way,
and for their iniquities.
18 All food was loathsome to them;
they reached the gates of death.
19 In their adversity they cried to the LORD
and He saved them from their troubles.
20 He gave an order and healed them;
He delivered them from the pits.[a]
21 Let them praise the LORD for His steadfast love,
His wondrous deeds for mankind.
22 Let them offer thanksgiving sacrifices,
and tell His deeds in joyful song.

[a] *Viz. of death*

23 Others go down to the sea in ships,
ply their trade in the mighty waters;
24 they have seen the works of the LORD
and His wonders in the deep.
25 By His word He raised a storm wind
that made the waves surge.
26 Mounting up to the heaven,
plunging down to the abyss,
disgorging in their misery,
27 they reeled and staggered like a drunken man,
all their skill to no avail.
28 In their adversity they cried to the LORD,
and He saved them from their troubles.
29 He made the storm subside;
the waves were stilled.
30 They rejoiced when all was quiet,
and He brought them to the port they desired.
31 Let them praise the LORD for His steadfast love,
His wondrous deeds for mankind.
32 Let them exalt Him in the congregation of the people,

praise Him in the assembly of the elders.

33 He turns the rivers into a wilderness,
springs of water into thirsty land,
34 fruitful land into a salt marsh,
because of the wickedness of its inhabitants.
35 He turns the wilderness into pools,
parched land into springs of water;
36 There He settles the hungry;
they build a place to settle in.
37 They sow fields and plant vineyards
that yield a fruitful harvest.
38 He blesses them and they increase greatly;
and He does not let their cattle decrease,
39 after they had been few and crushed
by oppression, misery and sorrow.
40 He pours contempt on great men
and makes them lose their way in trackless deserts;
41 but the needy He secures from suffering,
and increases their families like flocks.

42 The upright see it and rejoice;
the mouth of all wrongdoers is stopped.
43 The wise man will take note of these things;
he will consider the steadfast love of the LORD.

108 A song, a psalm of David.

2[a] My heart is firm, O God;
I will sing and chant a hymn with all my soul.
3 Awake, O harp and lyre!
I will wake the dawn.
4 I will praise You among the peoples, O LORD,
sing a hymn to You among the nations;
5 for Your faithfulness is higher than the heavens;
Your steadfastness reaches to the sky.
6 Exalt Yourself over the heavens, O God;
let Your glory be over all the earth!
7[b] That those whom You love may be rescued,
deliver with Your right hand and answer me.

8 God promised [c-]in His sanctuary[-c]
that I would exultingly divide up Shechem,
and measure the Valley of Sukkoth;

[a] *With vv. 2–6, cf. Ps. 57.8–12*

[b] *With vv. 7–14, cf. Ps. 60.7–14*

[c-c] *Or "by His holiness"*

9 Gilead and Manasseh would be mine,
Ephraim my chief stronghold,
Judah my scepter;
10 Moab would be my wash-basin;
on Edom I would cast my shoe;
I would raise a shout over Philistia.
11 Would that I were brought to the bastion!
Would that I were led to Edom!

12 But You have rejected us, O God;
God, You do not march with our armies.
13 Grant us Your aid against the foe,
for the help of man is worthless.
14 With God we shall triumph;
He will trample our foes.

109

For the leader.
A psalm of David.

O God of my praise,
do not keep aloof,
2 for the wicked and the deceitful
open their mouth against me;
they speak to me with lying tongue.
3 They encircle me with words of hate;
they attack me without cause.
4 They answer my love with accusation
[a-]and I must stand judgment.[-a]
5 They repay me with evil for good,
with hatred for my love.

6 Appoint a wicked man over him;
may an accuser stand at his right side;
7 may he be tried and convicted;
may he be judged and found guilty.
8 May his days be few;
may another take over [b-]his position.[-b]
9 May his children be orphans,
his wife a widow.
10 May his children wander from their hovels,
begging in search of [their bread].
11 May his creditor seize all his possessions;
may strangers plunder his wealth.
12 May no one show him mercy;

[a-a] Or "but I am all prayer"; meaning of Heb uncertain

[b-b] Meaning of Heb uncertain

may none pity his orphans;
13 may his posterity be cut off;
may their name be blotted out in the next generation.
14 May God be ever mindful of his father's iniquity,
and may the sin of his mother not be blotted out.
15 May the LORD be aware of them always
and cause their names to be cut off from the earth,
16 because he was not minded to act kindly,
and hounded to death the poor and needy man,
one crushed in spirit.
17 He loved to curse—may a curse come upon him!
He would not bless—may blessing be far from him!
18 May he be clothed in a curse like a garment,
may it enter his body like water,
his bones like oil.
19 Let it be like the cloak he wraps around him,
like the belt he always wears.
20 May the LORD thus repay my accusers,
all those who speak evil against me.

21 Now You, O GOD, my LORD,
act on my behalf as befits Your name.
Good and faithful as You are, save me.
22 For I am poor and needy,
and my heart is pierced within me.
23 I fade away like a lengthening shadow;
I am shaken off like locusts.
24 My knees give way from fasting;
my flesh is lean, has lost its fat.
25 I am the object of their scorn;
when they see me, they shake their head.
26 Help me, O LORD, my God;
save me in accord with Your faithfulness,
27 that men may know that it is Your hand,
that You, O LORD, have done it.
28 Let them curse, but You bless;
let them rise up, but come to grief,
while Your servant rejoices.
29 My accusers shall be clothed in shame,
wrapped in their disgrace as in a robe.

30 My mouth shall sing much praise to the LORD;
I will acclaim Him in the midst of a throng,
31 because He stands at the right hand of the needy,
to save him from those who would condemn him.

110 A psalm of David.

The LORD said to my lord,
"Sit at My right hand
while I make your enemies your footstool."

2 The LORD will stretch forth from Zion your mighty scepter;
hold sway over your enemies!
3 [a-]Your people come forward willingly on your day of battle.
In majestic holiness, from the womb,
from the dawn, yours was the dew of youth.[-a]

[a-a] *Meaning of Heb uncertain*

4 The LORD has sworn and will not relent,
"You are a priest forever, [b-]a rightful king by My decree."[-b]
5 The Lord is at your right hand.
He crushes kings in the day of His anger.

[b-b] *Or "after the manner of Melchizedek"*

6 He works judgment upon the nations,
heaping up bodies,
crushing heads far and wide.
7 He drinks from the stream on his way;
therefore he holds his head high.

111 Hallelujah.

א I praise the LORD with all my heart
ב in the assembled congregation of the upright.
ג 2 The works of the LORD are great,
ד [a-]within reach of all who desire them.[-a]
ה 3 His deeds are splendid and glorious;
ו His beneficence is everlasting;
ז 4 He has won renown for His wonders.
ח The LORD is gracious and compassionate;
ט 5 He gives food to those who fear Him;
י He is ever mindful of His covenant.
כ 6 He revealed to His people His powerful works,
ל in giving them the heritage of nations.
מ 7 His handiwork is truth and justice;
נ all His precepts are enduring,
ס 8 well-founded for all eternity,
ע wrought of truth and equity.
פ 9 He sent redemption to His people;
צ He ordained His covenant for all time;
ק His name is holy and awesome.

[a-a] *Meaning of Heb uncertain*

ר 10 The essence[b] of wisdom is the fear of the LORD;
ש [a-]all who practice it gain sound understanding.[-a]
ת Praise of Him is everlasting.

[b] Or "beginning"
[a-a] Meaning of Heb uncertain

112 Hallelujah.
א Happy is the man who fears the LORD,
ב who is greatly devoted to His commandments.
ג 2 His descendants will be mighty in the land,
ד a blessed generation of upright men.
ה 3 Wealth and riches are in his house,
ו and his beneficence lasts forever.
ז 4 [a-]A light shines[-a] for the upright in the darkness;
ח he is gracious, compassionate and beneficent.
ט 5 All goes well with the man who lends generously,
י who conducts his affairs with equity.
כ 6 He shall never be shaken;
ל the beneficent man will be remembered forever.
מ 7 He is not afraid of evil tidings;
נ his heart is firm, he trusts in the LORD.
ס 8 His heart is resolute, he is unafraid;
ע in the end he will see the fall of his foes.
פ 9 He gives freely to the poor;
צ his beneficence lasts forever;
ק his horn is exalted in honor.
ר 10 The wicked man shall see it and be vexed;
ש he shall gnash his teeth; his courage shall fail.
ת The desire of the wicked shall come to nothing.

[a-a] Or "He shines as a light"

113 Hallelujah.
O servants of the LORD, give praise;
praise the name of the LORD.
2 Let the name of the LORD be blessed
now and forever.
3 From east to west
the name of the LORD is praised.
4 The LORD is exalted above all nations;
His glory is above the heavens.
5 Who is like the LORD our God,
enthroned on high,
6 seeing what is below,
in heaven and on earth.
7 He raises the poor from the dust,
lifts up the needy from the refuse heap

8 to set them with the great,
with the great men of His people.
9 He sets the childless woman among her household
as a happy mother of children.
Hallelujah.

114

When Israel went forth from Egypt,
the house of Jacob from a people of strange speech,
2 Judah became His [a]holy one,[a]
Israel, His dominion.
3 The sea saw them and fled,
Jordan ran backward,
4 mountains skipped like rams,
hills like sheep.
5 What alarmed you, O sea, that you fled,
Jordan, that you ran backward,
6 mountains, that you skipped like rams,
hills, like sheep?
7 Tremble, O earth, at the presence of the LORD,
at the presence of the God of Jacob,
8 who turned the rock into a pool of water,
the flinty rock into a fountain.

[a-a] *Or "sanctuary"*

115

Not to us, O LORD, not to us
but to Your name bring glory
for the sake of Your love and Your faithfulness.
2 Why should the nations say,
"Where, now, is their God"
3 when our God is in heaven
and all that He wills He accomplishes?
4[a] Their idols are silver and gold,
the work of men's hands.
5 They have mouths, but cannot speak,
eyes, but cannot see;
6 they have ears, but cannot hear,
noses, but cannot smell;
7 they have hands, but cannot touch,
feet, but cannot walk;
they can make no sound in their throats.
8 Those who fashion them,
all who trust in them,
shall become like them.

[a] *With vv. 4–11, cf. 135.15–20*

9 O Israel, trust in the LORD!
He is their help and shield.
10 O house of Aaron, trust in the LORD!
He is their help and shield.
11 O you who fear the LORD, trust in the LORD!
He is their help and shield.

12 The LORD is mindful of us.
He will bless us;
He will bless the house of Israel;
He will bless the house of Aaron;
13 He will bless those who fear the LORD,
small and great alike.

14 May the LORD increase your numbers,
yours and your children's also.
15 May you be blessed by the LORD,
maker of heaven and earth.
16 The heavens belong to the LORD,
but the earth He gave over to man.
17 The dead cannot praise the LORD,
nor any who go down into silence.
18 But we shall bless the LORD
now and forever.
Hallelujah.

116

[a-]I love the LORD
for He hears[-a] my voice, my pleas;
2 for He turns His ear to me
whenever I call.
3 The bonds of death encompassed me;
the torments of Sheol overtook me.
I came upon trouble and sorrow
4 and I invoked the name of the LORD,
"O LORD, save my life!"

5 The LORD is gracious and beneficent;
our God is compassionate.
6 The LORD protects the simple;
I was brought low and He saved me.
7 Be at rest, once again, O my soul,
for the LORD has been good to you.
8 You[b] have delivered me from death,
my eyes from tears,

[a-a] Heb transposed for clarity. Others "I would love that the LORD hear," etc.

[b] I.e. God

my feet from stumbling.
9 I shall walk before the LORD
in the lands of the living.
10 [c]-I trust [in the LORD];
out of great suffering I spoke-[c]
11 and said rashly,
"All men are false."

[c-c] *Meaning of Heb uncertain*

12 How can I repay the LORD
for all His bounties to me?
13 I raise the cup of deliverance
and invoke the name of the LORD.
14 I shall pay my vows to the LORD
in the presence of all His people.
15 The death of His faithful ones
is grievous in the LORD's sight.

16 O LORD,
I am Your servant,
Your servant, the son of Your maidservant;
You have undone the cords that bind me.
17 I will sacrifice a thank-offering to You
and invoke the name of the LORD.
18 I will pay my vows to the LORD
in the presence of all His people,
19 in the courts of the house of the LORD,
in the midst of[d] Jerusalem.
Hallelujah.

[d] *Others "of you"*

117

Praise the LORD, all you nations;
extol Him, all you peoples,
2 for great is His steadfast love toward us;
the faithfulness of the LORD endures forever.
Hallelujah.

118

Praise the LORD for He is good,
His steadfast love is eternal.
2 Let Israel declare,
"His steadfast love is eternal."
3 Let the house of Aaron declare,
"His steadfast love is eternal."
4 Let those who fear the LORD declare,
"His steadfast love is eternal."

5 In distress I called on the LORD;
the Lord answered me and brought me relief.
6 The LORD is on my side,
I have no fear;
what can man do to me?
7 With the LORD on my side as my helper,
I will see the downfall of my foes.

8 It is better to take refuge in the LORD
than to trust in mortals;
9 it is better to take refuge in the LORD
than to trust in the great.

10 All nations have beset me;
by the name of the LORD I will surely [a-]cut them down.[-a]
11 They beset me, they surround me;
by the name of the LORD I will surely cut them down.
12 They have beset me like bees;
they shall be extinguished like burning thorns;
by the name of the LORD I will surely cut them down.

13 You[b] pressed me hard,
I nearly fell;
but the LORD helped me.
14 The LORD is my strength and might;[c]
He has become my deliverance.

15 The tents of the victorious[d] resound with joyous shouts of deliverance,
"The right hand of the LORD is triumphant!
16 The right hand of the LORD is exalted!
The right hand of the LORD is triumphant!"

17 I shall not die but live
and proclaim the works of the LORD.
18 The LORD punished me severely,
but did not hand me over to death.

19 Open the gates of victory[e] for me
that I may enter them and praise the LORD.
20 This is the gateway to the LORD—
the victorious[d] shall enter through it.

21 I praise You for You have answered me,
and have become my deliverance.
22 The stone which the builders rejected

[a-a] *Meaning of* 'amilam *in this and the following two verses uncertain*

[b] *I.e. the enemy*

[c] *Others "song"*

[d] *Or "righteous"*

[e] *Or "righteousness"*

has become the chief cornerstone.
23 This is the LORD's doing;
it is marvelous in our sight.
24 This is the day that the LORD has made—
let us exult and rejoice on it.

25 O LORD, deliver us!
O LORD, let us prosper!

26 Blessed is he who enters by the name of the LORD;
we bless you from the house of the LORD.
27 The LORD is God;
He has given us light;
[f]bind the festal offering to the horns of the altar with cords.[f]
28 You are my God and I will praise You;
You are my God and I will extol You.
29 Praise the LORD for He is good,
His steadfast love is eternal.

f-f Meaning of Heb uncertain

119

א

1 Happy are those whose way is blameless,
who follow the teaching of the LORD.
2 Happy are those who observe His decrees,
who turn to Him wholeheartedly.
3 They have done no wrong,
but have followed His ways.
4 You have commanded that Your precepts
be kept diligently.
5 Would that my ways were firm
in keeping Your laws;
6 then I would not be ashamed
when I regard all Your commandments.
7 I will praise You with a sincere heart
as I learn Your just rules.
8 I will keep Your laws;
do not utterly forsake me.

ב

9 How can a young man keep his way pure?—
by holding to Your word.
10 I have turned to You with all my heart;
do not let me stray from Your commandments.
11 In my heart I treasure Your promise;
therefore, I do not sin against You.
12 Blessed are You, O LORD;
train me in Your laws.

13 With my lips I rehearse
all the rules You proclaimed.
14 I rejoice over the way of Your decrees
as over all riches.
15 I study Your precepts;
I regard Your ways;
16 I take delight in Your laws;
I will not neglect Your word.

ג 17 Deal kindly with Your servant,
that I may live to keep Your word.
18 Open my eyes that I may perceive
the wonders of Your teaching.
19 I am only a sojourner in the land;
do not hide Your commandments from me.
20 My soul is consumed with longing
for Your rules at all times.
21 You blast the accursed insolent ones
who stray from Your commandments.
22 Take away from me taunt and abuse,
because I observe Your decrees.
23 Though princes meet and speak against me,
Your servant studies Your laws.
24 For Your decrees are my delight,
my intimate companions.

ד 25 My soul clings to the dust;
revive me in accordance with Your word.
26 I have declared my way, and You have answered me;
train me in Your laws.
27 Make me understand the way of Your precepts,
that I may study Your wondrous acts.
28 I am racked with grief;
sustain me in accordance with Your word.
29 Remove all false ways from me;
favor me with Your teaching.
30 I have chosen the way of faithfulness;
I have set Your rules before me.
31 I cling to Your decrees;
O LORD, do not put me to shame.
32 I eagerly pursue Your commandments,
for You broaden my understanding.

ה 33 Teach me, O LORD, the way of Your laws;
I will observe them [a]-to the utmost.-[a]

[a-a] *Meaning of Heb uncertain*

34 Give me understanding that I may observe Your teaching
and keep it wholeheartedly.
35 Lead me in the path of Your commandments,
for that is my concern.
36 Turn my heart to Your decrees
and not to love of gain.
37 Avert my eyes from seeing falsehood;
by Your ways preserve me.
38 Fulfill Your promise to Your servant,
which is for those who worship You.
39 Remove the taunt that I dread,
for Your rules are good.
40 See, I have longed for Your precepts;
by Your righteousness preserve me.

ו 41 May Your steadfast love reach me, O LORD,
Your deliverance, as You have promised.
42 I shall have an answer to those who taunt me,
for I have put my trust in Your word.
43 Do not utterly take the truth away from my mouth,
for I have put my hope in Your rules.
44 I will always obey Your teaching,
forever and ever.
45 I will walk about at ease
for I have turned to Your precepts.
46 I will speak of Your decrees,
and not be ashamed in the presence of kings.
47 I will delight in Your commandments,
which I love.
48 I reach out for Your commandments, which I love;
I study Your laws.

ז 49 Remember Your word to Your servant
through which You have given me hope.
50 This is my comfort in my affliction,
that Your promise has preserved me.
51 Though the arrogant have cruelly mocked me,
I have not swerved from Your teaching.
52 I remember Your rules of old, O LORD,
and find comfort in them.
53 I am seized with rage
because of the wicked who forsake Your teaching.
54 Your laws are [b-]a source of strength to me[-b]
wherever I may dwell.
55 I remember Your name at night, O LORD,

[b-b] *Or "my songs" with Targ.*

and obey Your teaching.
56 This has been my lot,
for I have observed Your precepts.

ח 57 The LORD is my portion;
I have resolved to keep Your words.
58 I have implored You with all my heart;
have mercy on me, in accordance with Your promise.
59 I have considered my ways,
and have turned back to Your decrees.
60 I have hurried and not delayed
to keep Your commandments.
61 Though the bonds of the wicked are coiled round me,
I have not neglected Your teaching.
62 I arise at midnight to praise You
for Your just rules.
63 I am a companion to all who fear You,
to those who keep Your precepts.
64 Your steadfast love, O LORD, fills the earth;
teach me Your laws.

ט 65 You have treated Your servant well,
according to Your word, O LORD.
66 Teach me good sense and knowledge,
for I have put my trust in Your commandments.
67 Before I was humbled I went astray,
but now I keep Your word.
68 You are good and beneficent;
teach me Your laws.
69 Though the arrogant have accused me falsely,
I observe Your precepts wholeheartedly.
70 Their minds are thick like fat;
as for me, Your teaching is my delight.
71 It was good for me that I was humbled,
so that I might learn Your laws.
72 I prefer the teaching You proclaimed
to thousands of gold and silver pieces.

י 73 Your hands made me and fashioned me;
give me understanding that I may learn Your commandments.
74 Your worshipers will see me and rejoice,
for I have put my hope in Your word.
75 I know, O LORD, that Your rulings are just;
rightly have You humbled me.
76 May Your steadfast love comfort me

in accordance with Your promise to Your servant.
77 May Your mercy reach me that I might live,
for Your teaching is my delight.
78 Let the insolent be dismayed for they have wronged me without cause;
I will study Your precepts.
79 May Your worshipers,
those who know Your decrees,
turn again to me.
80 May I wholeheartedly follow Your laws
so that I do not come to grief.

כ 81 I long for Your deliverance;
I hope for Your word.
82 My eyes pine away for Your promise;
I say, "When will You comfort me?"
83 Though I have become like a water-skin dried in smoke,
I have not neglected Your laws.
84 How long has Your servant to live?
when will You bring my persecutors to judgment?
85 The insolent have dug pits for me,
flaunting Your teaching.
86 All Your commandments are enduring;
I am persecuted without cause; help me!
87 Though they almost wiped me off the earth,
I did not abandon Your precepts.
88 As befits Your steadfast love, preserve me,
so that I may keep the decree You proclaimed.

ל 89 The LORD exists forever;
Your word stands firm in heaven.
90 Your faithfulness is for all generations;
You have established the earth and it stands.
91 They stand this day to [carry out] Your rulings,
for all are Your servants.
92 Were not Your teaching my delight,
I would have perished in my affliction.
93 I will never neglect Your precepts,
for You have preserved my life through them.
94 I am Yours; save me!
For I have turned to Your precepts.
95 The wicked hope to destroy me,
but I ponder Your decrees.
96 I have seen that all things have their limit,
but Your commandment is broad beyond measure.

מ 97 O how I love Your teaching!
It is my study all day long.
98 Your commandments make me wiser than my enemies;
they always stand by me.
99 I have gained more insight than all my teachers,
for Your decrees are my study.
100 I have gained more understanding than my elders,
for I observe Your precepts.
101 I have avoided every evil way
so that I may keep Your word.
102 I have not departed from Your rules,
for You have instructed me.
103 How pleasing is Your word to my palate,
sweeter than honey.
104 I ponder Your precepts;
therefore I hate every false way.

נ 105 Your word is a lamp to my feet,
a light for my path.
106 I have firmly sworn
to keep Your just rules.
107 I am very much afflicted;
O LORD, preserve me in accordance with Your word.
108 Accept, O LORD, my free-will offerings;
teach me Your rules.
109 Though my life is always in danger,
I do not neglect Your teaching.
110 Though the wicked have set a trap for me,
I have not strayed from Your precepts.
111 Your decrees are my eternal heritage;
they are my heart's delight.
112 I am resolved to follow Your laws
[a]-to the utmost-[a] forever.

[a-a] *Meaning of Heb uncertain*

ס 113 I hate men of divided heart,
but I love Your teaching.
114 You are my protection and my shield;
I hope for Your word.
115 Keep away from me, you evildoers,
that I may observe the commandments of my God.
116 Support me as You promised, so that I may live;
do not thwart my expectation.
117 Sustain me that I may be saved,
and I will always muse upon Your laws.
118 You reject all who stray from Your laws,

for they are false and deceitful.
119 You do away with the wicked as if they were dross;
rightly do I love Your decrees.
120 My flesh creeps from fear of You;
I am in awe of Your rulings.

ע 121 I have done what is just and right;
do not abandon me to those who would wrong me.
122 Guarantee Your servant's well-being;
do not let the arrogant wrong me.
123 My eyes pine away for Your deliverance,
for Your promise of victory.
124 Deal with Your servant as befits Your steadfast love;
teach me Your laws.
125 I am Your servant;
give me understanding
that I might know Your decrees.
126 It is a time to act for the LORD,
for they have violated Your teaching.
127 Rightly do I love Your commandments
more than gold, even fine gold.
128 Truly [c]by all [Your] precepts I walk straight;[c]
I hate every false way.

[c-c] *Or "I declare all [Your] precepts to be just"*

פ 129 Your decrees are wondrous;
rightly do I observe them.
130 The words [d]You inscribed[d] give light,
and grant understanding to the simple.
131 I open my mouth wide, I pant,
longing for Your commandments.
132 Turn to me and be gracious to me,
as is Your rule with those who love Your name.
133 Make my feet firm through Your promise;
do not let iniquity dominate me.
134 Redeem me from being wronged by man,
that I may keep Your precepts.
135 Show favor to Your servant,
and teach me Your laws.
136 My eyes shed streams of water
because men do not obey Your teaching.

[d-d] *With Targ.; meaning of Heb uncertain*

צ 137 You are righteous, O LORD;
Your rulings are just.
138 You have ordained righteous decrees;
they are firmly enduring.

139 I am consumed with rage
over my foes' neglect of Your words.
140 Your word is exceedingly pure,
and Your servant loves it.
141 Though I am belittled and despised,
I have not neglected Your precepts.
142 Your righteousness is eternal;
Your teaching is true.
143 Though anguish and distress come upon me
Your commandments are my delight.
144 Your righteous decrees are eternal;
give me understanding that I might live.

ק 145 I call with all my heart;
answer me, O LORD,
that I may observe Your laws.
146 I call upon You; save me,
that I may keep Your decrees.
147 I rise before dawn and cry for help;
I hope for Your word.
148 My eyes greet each watch of the night,
as I meditate on Your promise.
149 Hear my voice as befits Your steadfast love;
O LORD, preserve me, as is Your rule.
150 Those who pursue intrigue draw near;
They are far from Your teaching.
151 You, O LORD, are near,
and all Your commandments are true.
152 I know from Your decrees of old
that You have established them forever.

ר 153 See my affliction and rescue me,
for I have not neglected Your teaching.
154 Champion my cause and redeem me;
preserve me according to Your promise.
155 Deliverance is far from the wicked,
for they did not turn to Your laws.
156 Your mercies are great, O LORD;
as is Your rule, preserve me.
157 Many are my persecutors and foes;
I have not swerved from Your decrees.
158 I have seen traitors and loathed[e] them,
because they did not keep Your word in mind.
159 See that I have loved Your precepts;
O LORD, preserve me as befits Your steadfast love.

[e] *Or "have contended with"*

160 Truth is the essence of Your word;
Your just rules are eternal.

ש 161 Princes have persecuted me without reason;
my heart thrills at Your word.
162 I rejoice over Your promise
like one who obtains great spoil.
163 I hate and abhor falsehood;
I love Your teaching.
164 I praise You seven times each day
for Your just rules.
165 Those who love Your teaching enjoy well-being;
they encounter no adversity.
166 I hope for Your deliverance, O LORD;
I observe Your commandments.
167 I obey Your decrees
and love them greatly.
168 I obey Your precepts and decrees;
all my ways are before You.

ת 169 May my plea reach You, O LORD;
grant me understanding according to Your word.
170 May my petition come before You;
save me in accordance with Your promise.
171 My lips shall pour forth praise,
for You teach me Your laws.
172 My tongue shall declare Your promise,
for all Your commandments are just.
173 Lend Your hand to help me,
for I have chosen Your precepts.
174 I have longed for Your deliverance, O LORD;
Your teaching is my delight.
175 Let me live that I may praise You;
may Your rules be my help;
176 I have strayed like a lost sheep;
search for Your servant,
for I have not neglected Your commandments.

120

A song of Ascents.[a]

[a] *A term of uncertain meaning*

In my distress I called to the LORD
and He answered me.
2 O LORD, save me from treacherous lips,
from a deceitful tongue!

3 What can you profit,
what can you gain,
O deceitful tongue?
4 A warrior's sharp arrows,
with hot coals of broom-wood.

5 Woe is me, that I live with Meshech,
that I dwell among the clans of Kedar.
6 Too long have I dwelt with those who hate peace.
7 I am all peace;
but when I speak,
they are for war.

121 A song of Ascents.

I turn my eyes to the mountains;
from where will my help come?
2 My help comes from the LORD,
maker of heaven and earth.
3 He will not let your foot give way;
your guardian will not slumber;
4 See, the Guardian of Israel
neither slumbers nor sleeps!
5 The LORD is your guardian,
the LORD is your protection
at your right hand.
6 By day the sun will not strike you,
nor the moon by night.
7 The LORD will guard you from all harm;
He will guard your life.
8 The LORD will guard your going and coming
now and forever.

122 A song of Ascents.
[A psalm] of David.

I rejoiced when they said to me,
"We are going to the house of the LORD."
2 Our feet stood inside your gates, O Jerusalem,
3 Jerusalem built up, a city knit together,
4 to which tribes would make pilgrimage,
the tribes of the LORD,

—as was enjoined upon Israel—
to praise the name of the LORD.
5 There the thrones of judgment stood,
thrones of the house of David.
6 Pray for the well-being of Jerusalem;
may those who love you be at peace.
7 May there be well-being within your ramparts,
peace in your palaces.
8 For the sake of my kin and friends,
I pray for your well-being;
9 for the sake of the house of the LORD our God,
I seek your good.

123

A song of Ascents.

To You, enthroned in heaven,
I turn my eyes.
2 As the eyes of slaves follow their master's hand,
as the eyes of a slave-girl follow the hand of her mistress,
so our eyes are toward the LORD our God,
awaiting His favor.
3 Show us favor, O LORD,
show us favor!
We have had more than enough of contempt.
4 Long enough have we endured
the scorn of the complacent,
the contempt of the haughty.

124

A song of Ascents.
[A psalm] of David.

Were it not for the LORD who was on our side,
let Israel now declare,
2 were it not for the LORD who was on our side
when men assailed us,
3 they would have swallowed us alive
in their burning rage against us;
4 the waters would have carried us off,
the torrent would have swept over us;
5 over us would have swept
the seething waters.
6 Blessed is the LORD who did not let us
be ripped apart by their teeth.

7 We are like a bird escaped from the fowler's trap;
the trap broke and we escaped.
8 Our help is the name of the LORD,
maker of heaven and earth.

125 A song of Ascents.

Those who trust in the LORD
are like Mount Zion,
that cannot be moved,
enduring forever.
2 Jerusalem, hills enfold it,
and the LORD enfolds His people
now and forever.
3 [a-]The scepter of the wicked shall never rest
upon the land allotted to the righteous,
that the righteous not set their hand to wrongdoing.[-a]
4 Do good, O LORD, to the good,
to the upright in heart.
5 [a-]But those who in their crookedness act corruptly,[-a]
let the LORD make them go the way of evildoers.
May it be well with Israel!

a-a Meaning of Heb uncertain

126 A song of Ascents.

When the LORD restores the fortunes of Zion
[a-]—we see it in our dreams—[-a]
2 our mouths shall be filled with laughter,
our tongues, with songs of joy.
Then shall they say among the nations,
"The LORD has done great things for them!"
3 The LORD will do great things for us
and we shall rejoice.

4 Restore our fortunes, O LORD,
like watercourses in the Negeb.
5 They who sow in tears
shall reap with songs of joy.
6 Though he goes along weeping,
carrying the seed-bag,
he shall come back with songs of joy,
carrying his sheaves.

a-a Lit. "we are veritable dreamers"

127 A song of Ascents.
[A psalm] of Solomon.

Unless the LORD builds the house,
its builders labor on it in vain;
unless the LORD watches over the city,
the watchman keeps vigil in vain.
2 In vain do you rise early
and stay up late,
you who toil for the bread you eat;
[a]He provides as much for His loved ones while they sleep.[a]

[a-a] *Meaning of Heb uncertain*
[b] *Lit. "heritage"*

3 Sons are the provision[b] of the LORD;
the fruit of the womb, His reward.
4 Like arrows in the hand of a warrior
are sons born to a man in his youth.
5 Happy is the man who fills his quiver with them;
they shall not be put to shame
when they contend with the enemy in the gate.

128 A song of Ascents.

Happy are all who fear the LORD,
who follow His ways.
2 You shall enjoy the fruit of your labors;
you shall be happy and you shall prosper.
3 Your wife shall be like a fruitful vine within your house;
your sons, like olive saplings around your table.
4 So shall the man who fears the LORD be blessed.

5 May the LORD bless you from Zion;
may you share the prosperity of Jerusalem
all the days of your life,
6 and live to see your children's children.
May it be well with Israel!

129 A song of Ascents.

Since my youth they have often assailed me,
let Israel now declare,
2 since my youth they have often assailed me,
but they have never overcome me.

3 Plowmen plowed across my back;
they made long furrows.
4 The LORD, the Righteous One,
has snapped the cords of the wicked.

5 Let all who hate Zion
fall back in disgrace.
6 Let them be like grass on roofs
that fades before it can be pulled up,
7 that affords no handful for the reaper,
no armful for the gatherer of sheaves,
no exchange with passersby:
8 "The blessing of the LORD be upon you."
"We bless you by the name of the LORD."

130 A song of Ascents.

Out of the depths I call You, O LORD.
2 O Lord, listen to my cry;
let Your ears be attentive
to my plea for mercy.
3 If You keep account of sins, O LORD,
Lord, who will survive?
4 Yours is the power to forgive
so that You may be held in awe.

5 I look to the LORD;
I look to Him;
I await His word.
6 I am more eager for the Lord
than watchmen for the morning,
watchmen for the morning.

7 O Israel, wait for the LORD;
for with the LORD is steadfast love
and great power to redeem.
8 It is He who will redeem Israel from all their iniquities.

131 A song of Ascents.
[A psalm] of David.

O LORD, my heart is not proud
nor my look haughty;

I do not aspire to great things
or to what is beyond me;
2 [a]-but I have taught myself to be contented
like a weaned child with its mother;
like a weaned child am I in my mind.-[a]

[a-a] *Meaning of Heb uncertain*

3 O Israel, wait for the LORD
now and forever.

132 A song of Ascents.

O LORD, count in David's favor
his great self-denial,
2 how he swore to the LORD,
vowed to the Mighty One of Jacob,
3 "I will not enter my house,
nor will I mount my bed,
4 I will not give sleep to my eyes,
slumber to my eyelids[a]

[a] *Lit. "eyes"*

5 until I find a place for the LORD,
an abode for the Mighty One of Jacob."

6 We heard it was in Ephrath;
we came upon it in the region of Jaar.[b]

[b] *Cf. I Sam. 7.1–2; I Chron. 13.5–6*

7 Let us enter His abode,
bow at His footstool.
8 Advance, O LORD, to Your resting-place,
You and Your mighty ark!
9 Your priests are clothed in triumph;
Your loyal ones sing for joy.
10 For the sake of Your servant David
do not reject Your anointed one.

11 The LORD swore to David
a firm oath that He will not renounce,
"One of your own issue I will set upon your throne.
12 If your sons keep My covenant
and My decrees that I teach them,
then their sons also,
to the end of time,
shall sit upon your throne."
13 For the LORD has chosen Zion;
He has desired it for His seat.
14 "This is my resting-place for all time;
here I will dwell, for I desire it.

15 I will amply bless its store of food,
give its needy their fill of bread.
16 I will clothe its priests in victory,
its loyal ones shall sing for joy.
17 There I will make a horn sprout for David;
I have prepared a lamp for My anointed one.
18 I will clothe his enemies in disgrace,
while on him his crown shall sparkle."

133

A song of Ascents.
[A psalm] of David.

How good and how pleasant it is
that brothers sit together.
2 It is like fine oil on the head
running down onto the beard,
the beard of Aaron,
that comes down over the collar of his robe;
3 like the dew of Hermon
that falls upon the mountains of Zion.
There the LORD ordained blessing,
everlasting life.

134

A song of Ascents.

Now bless the LORD,
all you servants of the LORD,
who stand nightly
in the house of the LORD.
2 Lift your hands toward the sanctuary
and bless the LORD.
3 May the LORD,
maker of heaven and earth,
bless you from Zion.

135

Hallelujah.
Praise the name of the LORD;
give praise, you servants of the LORD
2 who stand in the house of the LORD,
in the courts of the house of our God.
3 Praise the LORD, for the LORD is good;
sing hymns to His name, for it is pleasant.

4 For the LORD has chosen Jacob for Himself,
Israel, as His treasured possession.

5 For I know that the LORD is great,
that our LORD is greater than all gods.
6 Whatever the LORD desires He does
in heaven and earth,
in the seas and all the depths.
7 He makes clouds rise from the end of the earth;
He makes lightning for the rain;
He releases the wind from His vaults.
8 He struck down the firstborn of Egypt,
man and beast alike;
9 He sent signs and portents against[a] Egypt,
against Pharaoh and all his servants;
10 He struck down many nations
and slew numerous kings—
11 Sihon king of the Amorites,
Og king of Bashan,
and all the royalty of Canaan—
12 and gave their lands as a heritage,
as a heritage to His people Israel.

13 O LORD, Your name endures forever,
Your fame, O LORD, through all generations;
14 for the LORD will champion His people,
and obtain satisfaction for His servants.

15[b] The idols of the nations are silver and gold,
the work of men's hands.
16 They have mouths, but cannot speak;
they have eyes, but cannot see;
17 they have ears, but cannot hear,
nor is there breath in their mouths.
18 Those who fashion them,
all who trust in them,
shall become like them.

19 O house of Israel, bless the LORD;
O house of Aaron, bless the LORD;
20 O house of Levi, bless the LORD;
you who fear the LORD, bless the LORD.
21 Blessed is the LORD from Zion,
He who dwells in Jerusalem.
Hallelujah.

[a] *Others "against you"*

[b] *With vv. 15–20, cf. 115.4–11*

136

Praise the LORD for He is good,
His steadfast love is eternal.
2 Praise the God of gods,
His steadfast love is eternal.
3 Praise the Lord of lords,
His steadfast love is eternal;
4 Who alone works great marvels,
His steadfast love is eternal;
5 Who made the heavens with wisdom,
His steadfast love is eternal;
6 Who spread the earth over the water,
His steadfast love is eternal;
7 Who made the great lights,
His steadfast love is eternal;
8 the sun to dominate the day,
His steadfast love is eternal;
9 the moon and the stars to dominate the night,
His steadfast love is eternal;
10 Who struck Egypt through their firstborn,
His steadfast love is eternal;
11 and brought Israel out of their midst,
His steadfast love is eternal;
12 with a strong hand and outstretched arm,
His steadfast love is eternal;
13 Who split apart the Sea of Reeds,
His steadfast love is eternal;
14 and made Israel pass through it,
His steadfast love is eternal;
15 Who hurled Pharaoh and his army into the Sea of Reeds,
His steadfast love is eternal;
16 Who led His people through the wilderness,
His steadfast love is eternal;
17 Who struck down great kings,
His steadfast love is eternal;
18 and slew mighty kings,—
His steadfast love is eternal;
19 Sihon king of the Amorites,
His steadfast love is eternal;
20 Og king of Bashan—
His steadfast love is eternal;
21 and gave their land as a heritage,
His steadfast love is eternal;
22 a heritage to His servant Israel,
His steadfast love is eternal;

23 Who took note of us in our degradation,
His steadfast love is eternal;
24 and rescued us from our enemies,
His steadfast love is eternal;
25 Who gives food to all flesh,
His steadfast love is eternal.
26 Praise the God of heaven,
His steadfast love is eternal.

137

By the rivers of Babylon,
there we sat,
sat and wept,
as we thought of Zion.
2 There on the poplars
we hung up our harps,
3 for our captors asked us there for songs,
our tormentors,[a] for amusement,
"Sing us one of the songs of Zion."
4 How can we sing a song of the LORD
on alien soil?
5 If I forget you, Jerusalem,
let my right hand wither;[b]
6 let my tongue stick to my palate
if I cease to think of you,
if I do not keep Jerusalem in memory
even at my happiest hour.

7 Remember, O LORD, against the Edomites
the day of Jerusalem's fall;
how they cried, "Strip her, strip her
to her very foundations!"
8 Fair Babylon, you predator,[c]
a blessing on him who repays you in kind
what you have inflicted on us;
9 a blessing on him who seizes your babies
and dashes them against the rocks!

[a] *Meaning of Heb uncertain*

[b] *Others "forget its cunning"*

[c] *With Targ.; others "who are to be destroyed"*

138

[A psalm] of David.

I praise You with all my heart,
sing a hymn to You among the divine beings;
2 I bow toward Your holy temple
and praise Your name for Your steadfast love and faithfulness,

because You have exalted Your name, Your word above all.

3 When I called, You answered me,
[a]You inspired me with courage.[a]

[a-a] *Meaning of Heb uncertain*

4 All the kings of the earth shall praise You, O LORD,
for they have heard the words You spoke.
5 They shall sing of the ways of the LORD,
"Great is the majesty of the LORD!"
6 High though the LORD is, He sees the lowly;
lofty, He perceives from afar.
7 Though I walk among enemies,
You preserve me in the face of my foes;
You extend Your hand;
with Your right hand You deliver me.
8 The LORD will settle accounts for me.
O LORD, Your steadfast love is eternal;
do not forsake the work of Your hands.

139

For the leader.
A psalm of David.

O LORD, You have examined me and know me.
2 When I sit down or stand up You know it;
You discern my thoughts from afar.
3 [a]You observe[a] my walking and reclining,
and are familiar with all my ways.

[a-a] *Meaning of Heb uncertain*

4 There is not a word on my tongue
but that You, O LORD, know it well.
5 You hedge me before and behind;
You lay Your hand upon me.
6 It is beyond my knowledge;
it is a mystery; I cannot fathom it.
7 Where can I escape from Your spirit?
Where can I flee from Your presence?
8 If I ascend to heaven, You are there;
if I descend to Sheol, You are there too.
9 If I take wing with the dawn
to come to rest on the western horizon,
10 even there Your hand will be guiding me,
Your right hand be holding me fast.
11 If I say, "Surely darkness [b]will conceal me,
night will provide me with cover."[b]

[b-b] *Cf. Rashi, Ibn Ezra; meaning of Heb uncertain*

12 Darkness is not dark for You;
night is as light as day;
darkness and light are the same.

13 It was You who created my conscience;[c]
You fashioned me in my mother's womb.
14 I praise You
for I am awesomely, wondrously made;
Your work is wonderful;
I know it very well.
15 My frame was not concealed from You
when I was shaped in a hidden place,
knit together in the recesses of the earth.
16 Your eyes saw my unformed limbs;
they were all recorded in Your book;
in due time they were formed,
[a-]to the very last one of them.[-a]
17 How weighty Your thoughts seem to me, O God,
how great their number!
18 I count them—they exceed the grains of sand;
I end—but am still with You.

19 O God, if You would only slay the wicked—
you murderers, away from me!—
20 [a-]who invoke You for intrigue,
Your enemies who swear by You falsely.[-a]
21 O LORD, You know I hate those who hate You
and loathe Your adversaries.
22 I feel a perfect hatred toward them;
I count them my enemies.

23 Examine me, O God, and know my mind;
probe me and know my thoughts.
24 See if I have vexatious ways,
and guide me in ways everlasting.

140

For the leader.
A psalm of David.

2 Rescue me, O LORD, from evil men,
save me from the lawless,
3 whose minds are full of evil schemes,
who incite wars every day.
4 They sharpen their tongues like serpents;
spiders' poison is on their lips. *Selah*

5 O LORD, keep me out of the clutches of the wicked;
save me from lawless men
who scheme to [a-]make me fall.[-a]

[c] *Lit. "kidneys"*

[a-a] *Meaning of Heb uncertain*

[a-a] *Lit. "push my feet"*

6 Arrogant men laid traps with ropes for me;
they spread out a net along the way;
they set snares for me. *Selah*

7 I said to the LORD: You are my God;
give ear, O LORD, to my pleas for mercy.
8 O GOD, my Lord, the strength of my deliverance,
You protected my head on the day of battle;[b]
9 O LORD, do not grant the desires of the wicked;
do not let their plan succeed,
[c-]else they be exalted. *Selah*

10 May the heads of those who beset me
be covered with the mischief of their lips;[-c]
11 may coals of fire drop down upon them,
and they be cast into pits, never to rise again.
12 Let slanderers have no place in the land;
[c-]let the evil of the lawless man hound him to destruction.[-c]
13 I know that the LORD will champion
the cause of the poor, the right of the needy.
14 Righteous men shall surely praise Your name;
the upright shall dwell in Your presence.

[b] *Lit. "arms"*

[c-c] *Meaning of Heb uncertain*

141 A psalm of David.

I call You, O LORD, hasten to me;
give ear to my cry when I call You.
2 Take my prayer as an offering of incense,
my upraised hands as an evening sacrifice.
3 O LORD, set a guard over my mouth,
a watch at the door of my lips;
4 let my mind not turn to an evil thing,
to practice deeds of wickedness
with men who are evildoers;
let me not feast on their dainties.
5[a] Let the righteous man strike me out of loyalty,
let him reprove me;
let my head not refuse such choice oil.
My prayers are still against their[b] evil deeds.
6 May their judges slip on the rock,
but let my words be heard, for they are sweet.
7 As when the earth is cleft and broken up
our bones are scattered at the mouth of Sheol.
8 My eyes are fixed upon You, O GOD my Lord;
I seek refuge in You, do not put me in jeopardy.

[a] *Meaning of vv. 5–7 uncertain*

[b] *I.e. the evildoers of v. 4*

9 Keep me from the trap laid for me,
and from the snares of evildoers.
10 Let the wicked fall into their nets
while I alone come through.

142

A *maskil* of David while he was in the cave.[a]
A prayer.

[a] *Cf. I Sam.* 24.3–4

2 I cry aloud to the LORD;
I appeal to the LORD loudly for mercy.
3 I pour out my complaint before Him;
I lay my trouble before Him
4 when my spirit fails within me.
You know my course;
they have laid a trap in the path I walk.
5 Look at my right and see—
I have no friend;
there is nowhere I can flee,
no one cares about me.
6 So I cry to You, O LORD;
I say, "You are my refuge,
all I have in the land of the living."
7 Listen to my cry, for I have been brought very low;
save me from my pursuers,
for they are too strong for me.
8 Free me from prison,
that I may praise Your name.
The righteous [b]shall glory in me[b]
for Your gracious dealings with me.

[b-b] *Meaning of Heb uncertain*

143

A psalm of David.

O LORD, hear my prayer;
give ear to my plea, as You are faithful;
answer me, as You are beneficent.
2 Do not enter into judgment with Your servant,
for before You no creature is in the right.

3 My foe hounded me;
he crushed me to the ground;
he made me dwell in darkness
like those long dead.
4 My spirit failed within me;
my mind was numbed with horror.

5 Then I thought of the days of old;
I rehearsed all Your deeds,
recounted the work of Your hands.
6 I stretched out my hands to You,
longing for You like thirsty earth. *Selah*

7 Answer me quickly, O LORD;
my spirit can endure no more.
Do not hide Your face from me,
or I shall become like those who descend into the Pit.
8 Let me learn of Your faithfulness by daybreak,
for in You I trust;
let me know the road I must take,
for on You I have set my hope.
9 Save me from my foes, O LORD;
[a-]to You I look for cover.[-a]
10 Teach me to do Your will,
for You are my God.
Let Your gracious spirit lead me
on level ground.
11 For the sake of Your name, O LORD, preserve me;
as You are beneficent, free me from distress.
12 As You are faithful, put an end to my foes;
destroy all my mortal enemies,
for I am Your servant.

[a-a] Meaning of Heb uncertain

144 [A psalm] of David.

Blessed is the LORD, my rock,
who trains my hands for battle,
my fingers for warfare;
2 my faithful one, my fortress,
my haven and my deliverer,
my shield, in whom I take shelter,
who makes peoples[a] subject to me.

[a] So Targ., Saadia; others "my people"

3 O LORD, what is man that You should care about him,
mortal man, that You should think of him?
4 Man is like a breath;
his days are like a passing shadow.
5 O LORD, bend Your sky and come down;
touch the mountains and they will smoke.
6 Make lightning flash and scatter them;
shoot Your arrows and rout them.

7 Reach Your hand down from on high;
rescue me, save me from the mighty waters,
from the hands of foreigners,
8 whose mouths speak lies,
and whose oaths[b] are false.

[b] *Lit. "right hand"*

9 O God, I will sing You a new song,
sing a hymn to You with a ten-stringed harp,
10 to You who gives victory to kings,
who rescues His servant David from the deadly sword.
11 Rescue me, save me from the hands of foreigners.
whose mouths speak lies,
and whose oaths[b] are false.

12[c] For our sons are like saplings,
well-tended in their youth;
our daughters are like cornerstones
trimmed to give shape to a palace.
13 Our storehouses are full,
supplying produce of all kinds;
our flocks number thousands,
even myriads in our fields;
14 our cattle are well cared for.
There is no breaching and no sortie,
and no wailing in our streets.

[c] *The meaning of several phrases in vv. 12–14 is uncertain*

15 Happy the people who have it so;
happy the people whose God is the Lord.

145 A song of praise; of David.

א I will extol You, my God and king,
and bless Your name forever and ever.
ב 2 Every day will I bless You
and praise Your name forever and ever.
ג 3 Great is the Lord and much acclaimed;
His greatness cannot be fathomed.
ד 4 One generation shall laud Your works to another
and declare Your mighty acts.
ה 5 The glorious majesty of Your splendor
and Your wondrous acts will I recite.
ו 6 Men shall talk of the might of Your awesome deeds,
and I will recount Your greatness.
ז 7 They shall celebrate Your abundant goodness,
and sing joyously of Your beneficence.

ח 8 The LORD is gracious and compassionate,
slow to anger and abounding in kindness.
ט 9 The LORD is good to all,
and His mercy is upon all His works.
י 10 All Your works shall praise You, O LORD,
and Your faithful ones shall bless You.
כ 11 They shall talk of the majesty of Your kingship,
and speak of Your might,
ל 12 to make His mighty acts known among men
and the majestic glory of His kingship.
מ 13 Your kingship is an eternal kingship;
Your dominion is for all generations.
ס 14 The LORD supports all who stumble,
and makes all who are bent stand straight.
ע 15 The eyes of all look to You expectantly,
and You give them their food when it is due.
פ 16 You give it openhandedly,
feeding every creature to its heart's content.
צ 17 The LORD is beneficent in all His ways
and faithful in all His works.
ק 18 The LORD is near to all who call Him,
to all who call Him with sincerity.
ר 19 He fulfills the wishes of those who fear Him;
He hears their cry and delivers them.
ש 20 The LORD watches over all who love Him,
but all the wicked will He destroy.
ת 21 My mouth shall utter the praise of the LORD,
and all creatures[a] shall bless His holy name forever and ever.

[a] *Lit. "flesh"*

146

Hallelujah.
Praise the LORD, O my soul!
2 I will praise the LORD all my life,
sing hymns to my God while I exist.

3 Put not your trust in the great,
in mortal man who cannot save.
4 His breath departs;
he returns to the dust;
on that day his plans come to nothing.

5 Happy is he who has the God of Jacob for his help,
whose hope is in the LORD his God,
6 maker of heaven and earth,
the sea and all that is in them;
who keeps faith forever;

7 who secures justice for those who are wronged,
gives food to the hungry.
The LORD sets prisoners free;
8 the LORD restores sight to the blind;
the LORD makes those who are bent stand straight;
the LORD loves the righteous;
9 the LORD watches over the stranger;
He gives courage to the orphan and widow,
but makes the path of the wicked tortuous.

10 The LORD shall reign forever,
your God, O Zion, for all generations.
Hallelujah.

147

Hallelujah.
It is good to chant hymns to our God;
it is pleasant to sing glorious praise.

2 The LORD rebuilds Jerusalem;
He gathers in the exiles of Israel.
3 He heals their broken hearts,
and binds up their wounds.
4 He reckoned the number of the stars;
to each He gave its name.
5 Great is our LORD and full of power;
His wisdom is beyond reckoning.
6 The LORD gives courage to the lowly,
and brings the wicked down to the dust.

7 Sing to the LORD a song of praise,
chant a hymn with a lyre to our God,
8 who covers the heavens with clouds,
provides rain for the earth,
makes mountains put forth grass;
9 who gives the beasts their food,
to the raven's brood what they cry for.
10 He does not prize the strength of horses,
nor value the fleetness[a] of men;
11 but the LORD values those who fear Him,
those who depend on His faithful care.

12 O Jerusalem, glorify the LORD;
praise your God, O Zion!
13 For He made the bars of your gates strong,
and blessed your children within you.

[a] *Lit. "thighs"*

14 He endows your realm with well-being,
and satisfies you with choice wheat.

15 He sends forth His word to the earth;
His command runs swiftly.
16 He lays down snow like fleece,
scatters frost like ashes.
17 He tosses down hail like crumbs—
who can endure His icy cold?
18 He issues a command—it melts them;
He breathes—the waters flow.
19 He issued His commands to Jacob,
His statutes and rules to Israel.
20 He did not do so for any other nation;
of such rules they knew nothing.
Hallelujah.

148

Hallelujah.
Praise the LORD, O you who are in heaven,
praise Him, O you who are in the heights.
2 Praise Him, all His angels,
praise Him, all His hosts.
3 Praise Him, sun and moon,
praise Him, all bright stars.
4 Praise Him, highest heavens,
and you waters that are above the heavens.
5 Let them praise the name of the LORD,
for it was He who commanded that they be created.
6 He made them endure forever,
establishing an order that shall never change.
7 Praise the LORD, O you who are on earth,
all sea monsters and ocean depths,
8 fire and hail, snow and smoke,
storm-wind that executes His command,
9 all mountains and hills,
all fruit trees and cedars,
10 all wild and tamed beasts,
creeping things and winged birds,
11 all kings and peoples of the earth,
all princes of the earth and its judges,
12 youths and maidens alike,
old and young together.
13 Let them praise the name of the LORD,
for His name, His alone, is sublime;

His splendor covers heaven and earth.
14 He has exalted the horn of His people
to the glory of all His faithful ones,
Israel, the people close to Him.
Hallelujah.

149

Hallelujah.
Sing to the LORD a new song,
His praises in the congregation of the faithful.
2 Let Israel rejoice in its maker;
let the children of Zion exult in their king.
3 Let them praise His name in dance;
with timbrel and lyre let them chant His praises.
4 For the LORD delights in His people;
He adorns the lowly with victory.
5 Let the faithful exult in glory;
let them shout for joy upon their couches,
6 with paeans to God in their throats
and two-edged swords in their hands,
7 to wreak vengeance upon the nations,
punishment upon the peoples,
8 binding their kings with shackles,
their nobles with chains of iron,
9 executing the doom decreed against them
to the glory of all His faithful.
Hallelujah.

150

Hallelujah.
Praise God in His sanctuary;
praise Him in the sky, His stronghold.
2 Praise Him for His mighty acts;
praise Him for[a] His exceeding greatness.
3 Praise Him with blasts of the horn;
praise Him with harp and lyre.
4 Praise Him with timbrel and dance;
praise Him with lute and pipe.
5 Praise Him with resounding cymbals;
praise Him with loud-clashing cymbals.
6 Let all that breathes praise the LORD.
Hallelujah.

[a] *Or "as befits"*